Uncle Tony's

Management Tips & Jokes

Wm. Allen

Published by

Harmony Books & Films, LLC
Suite 221B
602 W. Houstonia Ave.
Royal Oak, MI 48073
Text 248-894-0045

First Edition

Printed in the United States of America by Harmony Books & Films, LLC, Royal Oak, MI

Library of Congress Control Number: 2023948162
ISBN-13: 978-0990388678
ISBN-10: 0990388670

Copyeditor: Chris Doka
Front Cover Design: Wm Allen & Amnet Systems

Table of Contents

Table of Contents

Table of Contents

Foreword & Disclaimer

"It is quality rather than quantity that matters."

Source: Lucius Annaeus Seneca

This book suggests some practical leadership advice from a guy who always kept a low profile: Uncle Tony. He is not a CEO or famous management guru. He doesn't claim to know the leadership secrets of famous people from the past.

Uncle Tony didn't have much formal education, but he had a lot of common sense and knew how to deal with people. I never knew what Uncle Tony did for a living, since he never talked about his work. I just thought he was some sort of repairman, since people were always asking him to fix this or that. I found it surprising that a simple repairman like Uncle Tony knew so many people in high places.

It probably comes as no surprise: Uncle Tony wasn't big on putting things in writing. So, you aren't going to see any statistics or research studies in this book. He just had a natural feel for what would or would not work with people. He was a man of few words, so this book will be short and to the point.

I knew Uncle Tony before I was even a teenager and he died decades ago. So here I am in my seventies, trying to recall all the advice I received from Uncle Tony over the years. Hopefully, I have correctly recalled enough advice to make your management journey a little more successful—plus make life easier for those you report to and those who will report to you.

It never bothered Uncle Tony if people disagreed with him. He just tossed out his ideas, and people could take what made sense to them and forget the rest. He knew everyone was different and what works for one person may not work for another. I don't agree with everything he said nor should you. So please ignore any advice that you feel does not work for you.

I am just reporting what I can recall him saying over the years.

Wm. Allen

Topic 1: Action

"You are what you do,
not what you say you'll do."

Source: Carl Jung

Uncle Tony was never big on talking about what he was going to do; he just went out and did it. He thought talk will only get you so far. Sooner or later people are going to expect you to deliver.

Good ideas are wonderful. But if you don't act to make your ideas a reality, then it is the same as not having any ideas at all.

Sometimes you may have to do some things you would rather not do, such as speaking in public or asking for favors. Those kinds of things can be hard, especially for a guy like Uncle Tony. Other times, you may have to put your work ahead of things that you would rather do, like spending time with family and friends. No one gets to be a leader unless they are willing to make some sacrifices in order to become one.

Some of the actions you take will still go unnoticed or may even meet with disapproval. Don't get discouraged and give up. Learn from your mistakes and keep on trying. Eventually it will pay off, and even if it doesn't, at least you know you tried.

Uncle Tony once told me that he could teach me about action by just asking me a single question.

I said, "Go ahead."

Uncle Tony said, "Okay, there are five frogs on a log. One of them decides to jump off. How many are left?"

I replied, "That is easy, there are four left."

Uncle Tony said, "You are wrong. There are five left, because deciding isn't doing."

Topic 2: Advisors

"People inspire you, or they drain you.
Pick them wisely."

Source: Hans F. Hansen

Everyone needs advice, even Uncle Tony. But you don't want everyone to feel like they can offer you advice, or you will lose respect. Uncle Tony never wanted anyone to give him advice until he asked for it.

And you must make it clear that when you do ask for advice, it doesn't mean that you will take that advice. Remember that your own opinion is as good as, if not better than, that of the people advising you.

When you ask someone for advice, you need to make sure they feel comfortable telling you the truth, rather than something you want to hear. If you surround yourself with flatterers, such people can do you more harm than good.

And always be sure to thank your advisors for their advice, especially those whose advice you did not take or even liked.

When it comes to offering advice, I think you are on dangerous ground even if you ask the person first if they would like your advice.

I recall Uncle Tony telling me about a time when he was explaining a plan he had developed to some experts.

One of the experts asked Uncle Tony, "Would you like some advice?"

Uncle Tony said, "Sure."

The expert said, "It's bad."

Uncle Tony said, "That's okay, I'll listen to your advice anyway."

Topic 3: Affairs

"If we resist our passions,
it is more due to their weakness than our strength."

Source: Francois de la Rochefoucauld

The standard advice regarding romantic affairs at work is "don't." Few things can derail a career faster than an office romance. And please don't be so silly as to think no one will know you are having a workplace affair.

Something good coming out of a workplace affair becomes more unlikely the higher up you are in the organization. If the parties both work in the same department or if one reports to the other person, it becomes even more of a long shot. Uncle Tony never understood why when people know something is a long shot, they still bet things will turn out well.

If you believe the person is the "one," realize that most people think that. If you feel that way about this other person, there is little one can say to discourage you. Uncle Tony would just wish you the best and hope it works out for the both of you.

The real problem with office romances is when they don't work out, which is frequently common with any romance, not just office romances.

For example, Uncle Tony told me this story.

"I knew this guy, who was a department manager," said Uncle Tony. "On Fridays, at lot of his team members would stop off at a local bar and this one time after a particularly challenging week, he decided to join them."

I said, "So, what happened."

Uncle Tony said, "He and this woman had a little too much to drink and ended up hooking up for the night."

"Really," I said.

"Well, she starts coming in late three days in a row. So, the guy had no choice but to call her into his office." Uncle Tony added, "The manager apologized to the woman, saying they had both drank too much and it is just something that had happened. They needed to put this incident behind them and she needed to start showing up to work on time."

I asked, "What did she say?"

Uncle Tony said, "The woman said she was told that she could come into work whenever she felt like it. The manager wanted to know who told her that."

I said, "Yes, who would tell her such a thing?"

Uncle Tony said, "The woman told the manager that her attorney told her that."

Topic 4: Apology

"Never ruin an apology with an excuse."

Source: Benjamin Franklin

You are going to make mistakes; everyone makes them. The difference is that some people are big enough to apologize for their mistakes, while others can't admit they were wrong.

To help these people who cannot bring themselves to apologize, Uncle Tony told them that apologizing was a good way for them to have the last word. That was Uncle Tony, always trying to help even the undeserving.

You should own up to your mistakes, whether it was an error in judgment or the way you treated someone. As soon as you realize you have done wrong, make an apology right away. However, if your apology isn't sincere, you are better off not making it. People can always detect a phony apology.

On the other side of the coin, always be gracious in accepting an apology, even an insincere one.

Speaking of apologies, I recall Uncle Tony telling me that he felt bad for calling a guy stupid.

I said, "So did you apologize?"

Uncle Tony said, "Yes, I made a sincere apology to the fellow. But he refused to accept my apology."

I asked, "How did you apologize to the fellow?"

Uncle Tony replied, "I said that I'm sorry I offended you when I called you stupid, but I thought you already knew."

Topic 5: Appraisals

"The most basic problem is that performance appraisals
often don't accurately assess performance."

Source: W. Edwards Deming

Perhaps Mr. Deming should have added to the above quote, "and often decreases performance." Other than your top performers, you are lucky if the rest of your team will perform as well as they did before they received their evaluation. Uncle Tony thought the big problem with written appraisals is the negative comment. You can say nine positive comments and one negative comment and yet when the person goes home, the only thing on their mind will be that negative comment.

No matter how one feels about performance appraisals, if you are in a corporation that calls for them, then you have to do them. Your goal should be to get the process over as quickly and painlessly as possible.

Self-appraisals are the way to go. However, guidelines must be in place so team members can evaluate their own performance; otherwise, the process is very subjective. Most team members are modest, so you will often end up adding positive comments and toning down negative comments. Occasionally, you will come across a person whose self-appraisal has no relationship to reality. This is why it is important that detailed performance guidelines are in place.

If you are on the receiving end of an appraisal, especially a bad one, I urge you to graciously accept the appraisal with a simple "thank you for the feedback." Getting angry will not help your situation. On reflection, you may find some changes in yourself are necessary.

I knew Uncle Tony hated performance appraisals, so one day, I asked him why.

He said, "Because they usually say something bad about you."

I asked, "What could anyone say bad about you?"

Uncle Tony said, "My boss gave me an appraisal and it described my work performance as hitting rock bottom."

I asked, "Didn't it say anything positive?"

Uncle Tony replied, "Yeah, it said that although my performance has hit rock bottom, I still keep digging."

Topic 6: Arguments

"A man convinced against his will,
is of the same opinion still."

Source: Dale Carnegie

Arguments are common when people work together. A leader needs to make sure these arguments stay respectful. You don't want an argument to go on so long that it hurts the team. A leader must stop long-running arguments, even if it means removing a team member.

As for you getting involved in arguments, it is impossible to win an argument, so avoid them. If you do get in arguments, please don't try to win every argument. To do so is a big mistake, since not every battle is worth winning. I recall Uncle Tony telling me a story about the Alamo. He said that after the Battle of the Alamo, one of Santa Anna's generals said, "We can't afford to win another battle like this."

The person with the opposing view isn't likely to be stupid, and if you were in their position, you might think the same thing. Uncle Tony said "Where we stand on an issue often depends upon where we happen to be sitting. When we change seats, we often change our position on things."

If you must disagree with someone, do so with tact and in a way that allows the other person to save face. And you never want to become angry during an argument, since you will likely end up looking stupid.

Speaking of arguments, Uncle Tony told me that one time he got into an argument with his furnace.

I asked, "What happened?"

Uncle Tony said, "Well, things got a little heated."

Topic 7: Ask

"If you don't ask,
the answer is always no."

Source: Nora Roberts

If you think you're going to get a promotion by working hard and delivering, that will often not be the case.

You usually have to ask, and the best way to ask is by saying what you can deliver going forward. That will work far better than talking about what you have accomplished in the past. You should only mention the past to make a convincing argument of what you can deliver in the future.

Do not associate your request with a threat. No one likes to be threatened. They will either take you up on your challenge or give in but not like you.

I recall asking Uncle Tony if he had any advice on asking for a raise or a promotion.

"Well, what I did was to just walk up to the boss and demand a promotion; otherwise, I said I was quitting this crummy company," replied Uncle Tony.

I said, "Wow, and did you get what you wanted?"

Uncle Tony said, "Yeah, I didn't want to work there anyways."

Topic 8: Attitude

"Your problem isn't the problem,
it's your attitude about the problem."

Source: Ann Brashares

Uncle Tony thought attitude was everything. Stay positive, regardless of what you are experiencing. Usually, you can find some good in the worst of situations. If you feel the situation is so bad that you have to leave your job, well the good news is that the situation has inspired you to find a better position.

A good attitude also consists of being flexible and willing to meet the needs of the corporation. If you have to go on a business trip, agree with a smile on your face. Same thing if you have to come in on weekends or holidays. If you have to do it, you might as well do it with a smile.

Your own positive attitude will serve as a role model to your team. You can do this in ways that demonstrate you value their contributions, recognize their talents, and have confidence in them. It is good that you think well of your team; but most important, you must do everything you can to make sure that they think well of themselves. If your team believes they are the best, they will be the best. People tend to live up to their beliefs.

Most important of all, you need to have passion for what you are doing. Uncle Tony always loved repeating this story about the building of a cathedral during the Middle Ages as an example of the attitude that makes a person successful:

A man came across three masons who were working at chipping chunks of granite from large blocks.

The first seemed unhappy at his job, chipping away and often looking at his watch. When the man asked what it was that he was doing, the first mason replied, "I'm hammering this stupid rock, and I can't wait 'til 5 when I can go home."

The man asked a second mason, who was carefully hammering the granite block, what he was doing. The mason replied, "Well, I'm molding this block of rock so that it can be used with others to construct a wall. It's not bad work, but I'll sure be glad when it's done."

A third mason was passionately hammering at his block, taking time to stand back and admire his work. He chipped off small pieces until he was satisfied that it was the best he could do. When asked what he was doing, the mason stopped, looked upward, and proudly said, "I am building a cathedral!"

Topic 9: Benchmarks

"Copy cats may seem good at what they are doing,
but they will never find a spot at the top."

Source: Cyc Jouzy

Benchmarking is useful for your company and for you. You need to know the best practices of your peers, both inside and outside your company. Find those who are doing your work better than you and learn from them.

However, Uncle Tony was never a fan of benchmarking. It didn't make sense to him that someone would give away their best practices without getting something in return. He thought sharing a best practice with everyone would soon turn it into nothing more than a standard practice.

He thought if you wanted to come up with a cool idea, you needed to look at work that is much different from your own. For example, he had heard that the fast-food industry came up with drive-in windows from Formula 1 pit stops.

Uncle Tony told me, "I used this same concept to come up with an idea of a belt made entirely of watches."

I asked, "What became of that idea?"

Uncle Tony said, "I thought about it and decided it was a waist of time."

Topic 10: Blame

"A good leader takes a little more of his share of the blame,
and a little less of his share of the credit."

Source: Arnold H. Glasow

Uncle Tony said that you should never be afraid to accept the blame for any failure, even if the failure is not directly your fault. He thought it was all about being responsible.

Actually, being willing to accept blame puts you in the seat of power, since you are the one accepting responsibility. Plus, you have probably brought some relief to someone.

And when you are in charge, all blame stops at your desk; you cannot permit it to pass down to anyone on your team. Otherwise, it is not only unfair to your team members, but it makes you look weak in everyone's eyes.

One time an interviewer told Uncle Tony, "We are looking for someone who is responsible."

Uncle Tony said, "I'm your guy. Just check with my last employer."

The interviewer said, "And what are they going to tell me?"

Uncle Tony said, "They will tell you that every time something went wrong, I was responsible."

Topic 11: Boldness

"Be bold and mighty forces will come to your aid."

Source: Goethe

Uncle Tony thought one cannot advance by being timid. If you are timid, even your supporters will be reluctant to support you.

As Goethe points out in the above quote, boldness often brings help from unexpected sources. However, the boldness that brings success comes from your knowledge that you can accomplish something that others would not even try. Boldness is not simply foolish risk-taking.

On the other hand, if you feel something is wrong, regardless of how much pressure you are under to go along, be bold enough to not do it.

Uncle Tony loved to tell jokes. I recall years ago he told me one related to this topic:

Uncle Tony said, "Two fonts walked into a bar."

The bartender said, "Hey, we don't serve fonts in this bar!"

The fonts sat down anyway.

Uncle Tony asked me, "Do you know why the two fonts did that?"

I replied, "I have no idea."

Uncle Tony said, "Because those two fonts were bold."

Topic 12: Budgets

"The simplest definition of a budget is
telling your money where to go."

Source: Tsh Oxenreider

Many corporations do not have an enlightened budget process. If you are in such a corporation, which is most likely, then the budgeting process is a necessary evil that you must go through. Your goal, said Uncle Tony, should be to spend as little time as possible on the budget process. If your area had a prior-year budget, your best approach is probably to modify it a little.

Always appear as if you are taking the budgeting process seriously. You want to work as much padding as possible into your budget; otherwise, you will spend more hours explaining why you are over budget.

Make sure your spending conforms to the approved budget. Some corporations expect you to spend half your budget in the first six months. If you don't, they will try to take back the unspent portion of the first half of your budget. You may be able to avoid this situation by designating in advance that you will be spending the bulk of your budget in the second half of the year.

There is the chance that you will find yourself in a corporation that has an enlightened budget process. If so, you will want to take time on your budget to spell out your vision for your area. This will include seeking input from your team and those outside of your team whom you consider to be visionaries.

Your goal is a budget that says where you are, where you want to be, how you plan to get there, and the cost of getting there. All stated as realistically and in as much detail as possible.

The world is a changing place and as time goes on, things may take place that will impact your budget. In which case, you should request, with detailed rationale, a budget variance at the first sign of a budget overrun.

Hopefully, you find yourself in this enlightened corporate world. If not, play the game as well as possible, without wasting too much of your time.

Although Uncle Tony was not fond of the typical corporate budget process, he did tell me there was one time when he found it useful.

I said, "Knowing how much you dislike the corporate budget process, I want to hear how you found it useful?"

Uncle Tony said, "Well, one time at work, my wife appears unexpectedly and walks into my office, which was awkward."

I said, "How so?"

"Well, my secretary was sitting on my lap and I was talking on the phone when my wife walked in."

I asked, "So, what did you do?"

Uncle Tony replied, "I said into the phone, I don't care about these budget cuts, I cannot continue to run this office with only one chair."

Topic 13: Campaign

"I've learned that people will forget what you said,
people will forget what you did,
but people will never forget how you made them feel."

Source: Maya Angelou

You might think running a campaign is just for politicians, but you are wrong.

Every day in the corporate world is an opportunity to campaign like you were running for election. You must make everyone you come into contact with feel better about themselves and what they are doing than they did before they met you. You do this not only with your words, but also your actions. For instance, when someone walks up to you and you are seated, stand up. When you make others feel better about themselves, they will think better about you.

You need to make everyone, from the highest to the lowest level employee, feel like they are the most important person you have ever met. Don't leave executives out of your campaign. Even executives appreciate it when people notice things they have done well. And while you're at it, don't forget making your peers feel good about themselves and what they are doing.

However, when you praise someone, be as specific as possible. Otherwise, it will simply seem like false praise. If you are on the receiving end of false praise, it is probably best to simply say thank you.

Uncle Tony told me once he was waiting for a man of importance about a business deal.

Uncle Tony told one of his lieutenants, "A man of importance will be stopping by and under no circumstance, let the man leave before I get back. I'll only be gone a few minutes."

The lieutenant said, "How will I know who he is?"

Uncle Tony replied, "He will be the nicest person you have ever met in your life."

Uncle Tony told me that later in the day, his lieutenant came up to him and said, "You're right, he was the nicest person I had ever met."

Topic 14: Celebrate

"The more you praise and celebrate your life,
the more there is in life to celebrate."

Source: Oprah Winfrey

Uncle Tony believed in celebrating both large and small accomplishments of everyone. He thought celebrations motivated people, although he was very low-key about his own successes and preferred to celebrate those discreetly.

It wasn't unusual for Uncle Tony to make a bigger deal out of an associate's accomplishment than they did themselves. He did this not only to those who reported to him, but also for peers. He was always careful to keep the celebrations appropriate with the accomplishment or occasion. He thought over-the-top celebrations come across as insincere.

Uncle Tony would also try to find a way to celebrate the accomplishments or special occasions of his superiors, but he always approached this with a great deal of care, as it could be viewed as nothing more than an attempt to win favor.

In addition to celebrating people's business accomplishments, he made it a point to acknowledge people's birthdays, employment anniversaries, and weddings (including weddings of their children).

Uncle Tony told me about the time he took his first wife to a wedding, just before they were to be divorced.

I asked, "What happened?"

Uncle Tony said, "There was some guy on the dance floor doing back flips, the splits, you name it and he was doing it."

I said, "So?"

Uncle Tony said, "Well, my wife says to me, you know, 15 years ago that guy asked me to marry him and I turned him down."

I said, "So what did you say to her?"

Uncle Tony said, "I told her that it looks like he is still celebrating."

Topic 15: Change

"God grant me the serenity
to accept the things I cannot change,
courage to change the things I can,
and the wisdom to know the difference."

Source: *Serenity Prayer* composed by Reinhold Niebuhr

Uncle Tony used to say, "Unlike a vending machine, you can always count on change in the corporate world."

Another thing you can count on in the corporate world is if you resist change, your career is going nowhere. Besides, it is easier to go along with the change than it is to resist it.

True, often change can be no more than a return to a past practice by new leadership, but it is still change. It can also be change caused by technology or new competition. Don't be foolish and try to cling to the past, simply embrace the new quickly and enthusiastically. You only have two choices: accept the change or find another position.

The best strategy for implementing your own change is to get those impacted by the change involved in designing the change. If you are a master change agent, those involved may come to believe the change is their idea and that you are merely approving their change.

If the change is associated with you and not those impacted, you are likely to find those benefiting from the old way will strongly resist the change. As for those who might benefit from your change, their support will likely be lukewarm. Therefore, you want to downplay the change as much as possible to those impacted by the change. Try to make it appear that the change is no big deal. Also, reassure people if the change is of no benefit, you'll go back to the old method.

Speaking of change, Uncle Tony asked me, "How many psychiatrists does it take to change a light bulb?"

I said, "I don't know."

Uncle Tony said, "Just one, but the light bulb has to want to change."

Topic 16: Clothing

"Clothing is ultimately the suit of armor in which we
battle the world."

Source: Sophia Amoruso

Uncle Tony believed that your clothing choices were a form of communication. He would suggest you ask yourself if your clothing choices say, "I'm ready for the next level." Do they say you will fit in with that next level?

Your clothing choices can also impact your self-image. Select clothes that make you feel like the person you want to be.

Look at how the people who are one level above you dress and use that as your guide. Remember your clothing choices not only say who you are, but who you want to be.

Uncle Tony always said there was nothing sadder than someone coming into work dressed better than usual and people saying, "You must be interviewing today." Why would someone interested in advancement feel compelled to dress differently for an interview than they normally dress? Always remember you are interviewing every day, whether or not you have a scheduled interview.

Speaking of clothing, Uncle Tony asked me, "Do you know what is an attorney's favorite article of clothing?"

I said, "I don't know."

Uncle Tony said, "Lawsuits."

Topic 17: Co-Workers

"There are people who take the heart out of you,
and there are those who put it back."

Source: Elizabeth David

Uncle Tony believed that you should support all your co-workers, both the talented and the struggling. It is what a nice person does and what someone who just wants to get ahead should do.

If your co-workers aren't up to the job, never complain about them or say anything negative about them. Their work will speak for itself, without you pointing it out. You may even want to defend them by saying they are trying, but only if they are trying. However, it is a mistake to compliment the quality of their work to higher-ups, since the higher-ups will eventually find out the truth about these people and think you are a bad judge of talent.

Incompetent co-workers make you look good, unless you are their boss. If they are good people, you should try helping them. Uncle Tony thought you should remember your goal is climbing the corporate ladder, not harming people. Plus, he thought it is a great way to gain supporters for your corporate climb.

You will at times come across co-workers who are superior to you. That is good.

Uncle Tony liked the saying, "If you are the smartest person in the room, then it is time to find a different room."

Superior co-workers will motivate you to work harder and smarter, and push you to up your game. Become their friend and learn from them. There is a good possibility they may assist you up the corporate ladder, if your friendship with them is sincere.

Speaking of co-workers, Uncle Tony said, "One time I told my hot co-worker how I felt."

I said, "That's totally inappropriate."

Uncle Tony replied, "Well maybe, but it turns out that she felt the same way as I did, so we turned on the air conditioner."

Topic 18: Coach

"Coaching is unlocking a person's potential
to maximize their growth."

Source: John Whitmore

If you are in leadership, one of your roles is to coach your team members. However, even if you aren't yet in leadership, you should still be willing to coach your peers if your help is welcomed. Don't be afraid that if you help them, their performance will outshine your performance.

Uncle Tony would encourage you to be a person who is not afraid to help a teammate. If you want to rise up in the organization, help others, and it is likely they will applaud your climb up the corporate ladder and may even support that climb.

It is likely you have heard about focusing on correcting a person's weaknesses. Don't expect this approach to go over well. I think most people find perfecting their strengths more natural and enjoyable than trying to eliminate their flaws. Plus, working on one's strengths will be of more benefit to both the organization and the individual. It is difficult for anyone to correct their weaknesses, even when they want to change.

I was surprised, when Uncle Tony told me I should not try at home some of the tips these business coaches recommend.

I asked him, "Why?"

He said, "I was in a class and this business coach was telling us the different ways to spot things that could be made more efficient."

I asked, "Did the tips work?"

Uncle Tony said, "Oh, they worked alright."

I said, "Well, what is the problem?"

Uncle Tony said, "I was watching how my wife made breakfast for us and it was taking her twenty minutes to make breakfast. So I gave her some tips."

I said, "I still don't see the problem, you said the tips worked."

Uncle Tony said, "Yeah, they worked. Now I'm making our breakfast in ten minutes."

Topic 19: Communication

"Wise men speak because they have something to say,
fools because they have to say something."

Possible Source: Plato

The first rule in communications, whether it is oral or written, is that less is more. What you want to express will get lost in a lot of verbiage, so be concise.

For instance, Uncle Tony asked, "Do you know anything about Edward Everett?"

I admitted I did not.

Uncle Tony said, "I'm not surprised, hardly anyone knows about him. Edward Everett is the fellow that gave a two-hour speech at Gettysburg before Lincoln came up and gave his less than three-minute speech."

Yes, being concise takes more effort than being verbose; but it is worth the effort if you wish to get your message across. I'm not sure if it is true, but I've heard you can only expect a reader to read two pages of a letter closely.

If you wish to get ahead in the business world, not only is it important to communicate well in writing, but you must also speak in public. And when you do, please don't be boring. Your audience will very quickly decide if you are worth listening to, so you need to start off strong. And when speaking, be sure to not speak too long. You always want to have your audience wishing you had spoken longer.

If you are afraid to speak in public or can't speak without being boring, your best approach is to be as brief as possible. Perhaps, you should limit your talk to simply introducing someone who will explain the topic in detail.

Most people don't even pay attention to what you say. Once, Uncle Tony told me a story about President Teddy Roosevelt.

Uncle Tony said, "President Roosevelt grew tired of exchanging mindless pleasantries with people he would be introduced to at formal gatherings.

As time went on, President Roosevelt, when being introduced to people, would say, 'I murdered my grandmother this morning.'

Upon hearing President Roosevelt's confession, no one paid the slightest attention, until one elderly gentleman leaned over and whispered in President Roosevelt's ear, 'I'm sure she had it coming.'"

Topic 20: Compliment

"A compliment is verbal sunshine."

Source: Robert Orben

You want to be the source of sunshine so always make sure you give far more compliments than you receive. Make sure they are sincere and recognize something. Uncle Tony thought you always needed to explain why you think it was nice work. Instead of just saying, "Nice report," you could say, "Citing your sources made your report look very professional."

We all like receiving compliments. When someone gives you a compliment, don't play down your worth. Simply say thank you.

Once in a while, give yourself a compliment. But do so carefully so you don't look like a bragger. It is one thing to discretely compliment yourself; but it is bad form to solicit compliments.

I remember Uncle Tony telling me about a time when he walked into a bar and sat down.

A bowl of popcorn said, "You look like a cool guy."

Uncle Tony thought it must have just been his imagination.

The bartender asked Uncle Tony what he wanted and Uncle Tony ordered a rum and coke. The bartender turned away to get the drink.

The popcorn said, "Excellent choice."

The talking popcorn was freaking Uncle Tony out. Soon, the bartender returned.

Uncle Tony asked, "Hey, what's with this talking popcorn?"

The bartender replied, "Don't worry about it, the popcorn is complimentary."

Topic 21: Compromise

"Compromise is not about losing.

It is about deciding that the other person has just as much right to be happy with the end result as you do."

Source: Donna Martini

You have probably heard it said that when you compromise, you lose. Even Uncle Tony used to say, "A compromise is when both parties get what they don't want." Nevertheless, Uncle Tony could always come up with a compromise that people would accept, even if they weren't thrilled with the outcome.

There are some who recommend going into a negotiation with extremely high demands and sticking with those demands as long as possible. The idea is to wear down your opponent until they simply agree. If they don't simply agree, perhaps they will say, "Let's split the difference," which works out well for the party with the excessive demands. But honestly, is this who you want to be?

When it comes to compromising, here are a few things to think about:

We should never compromise our core principles, since this will cause people to question our integrity. It is like they say, if you don't stand for something, you will fall for anything.

However, most things are not about your core values and if you refuse to compromise, you will be jeopardizing your personal and business relationships. For example, Uncle Tony said, "When it comes to marriage, you can either be right or happy."

As for long-standing business relationships, you had better do some compromising if you want to keep that relationship. I recall Uncle Tony saying, "Who wants to do business with someone whose idea of a compromise is that they get their way, and you have to find a way to be okay with that?"

Be the person who doesn't take advantage of anyone nor lets anyone take advantage of them.

Talking about compromising, Uncle Tony asked me, "What is it called when two spiritualists reach a compromise?"

I said, "I don't know."

Uncle Tony said, "A happy medium."

Topic 22: Conversation

"A lot of people understand what not saying anything means, so, in effect, not saying anything is really saying a lot."

Source: Bill Walton

Your own words will likely do you more harm than the words of anyone else. Also, your own words can hurt others, so think before you speak. Look around, see who is there, realize what you say will likely be passed on to those not present. And don't say anything in writing or electronic communications that you would not want to see printed in the newspaper.

Finally, whenever you give your word, keep it. Uncle Tony was fond of quoting Napoleon, who said, "The best way to keep one's word is not to give it."

Try to say nothing definite or include caveats in your statements, such as "based upon what I know at the moment," or better yet phrase your statement as a question. Best of all, try to say as little as possible about your opinions, history, plans, etc. Remember, once something is said, it cannot be taken back. You are much better off simply listening to others more than saying something yourself.

I am not suggesting that you remain silent. At times, saying nothing is as bad, if not worse, than saying too much. For you to say nothing can imply you are in agreement with what is being said. For example, you may want to defend someone who is being talked about but is not there to defend themselves.

Everyone knew Uncle Tony was a man of few words. Once, a girl sat next to him and said that she made a bet that she could get Uncle Tony to say three words.

Uncle Tony said, "You lose."

Topic 23: Costs

"Watch the costs
and
the profits will take care of themselves."

Source: Andrew Carnegie

One of the best ways to hold down costs is to make sure everything you and your team are doing is necessary. You also want a bidding process for selecting vendors or at least some method to make sure the cost of goods and services is reasonable.

Once in a while you may come across a big cost savings; but usually, your cost savings will come from small changes to a process that simply speeds things up. Encourage your team to look at what they do each day with fresh eyes to see if they can come up with a better way of doing things.

Uncle Tony thought a good way to control costs is to spend your corporation's money like it was your own. If you do that, odds are that you will be one of the top cost cutters in your corporation. That doesn't mean that you should be a miser, just that you should spend wisely. There are times when spending money will result in an overall cost reduction, or add significant benefits to the operation.

Uncle Tony used to say "costs walk in on two feet."

I asked him what he meant and he told me years ago he was running a small operation and was asked by his crew to bring in a part-time employee. He told me that it seemed a reasonable request. However, before long there was a request for a second phone, and before long other requests came in related to the part-time employee.

When you must cut costs that directly impact your team members, if at all possible, seek your team's advice. And when it comes to cost cutting, model the behavior by starting with yourself first. Let your team know about the cost cutting measures you have applied to yourself. This will make it all the more likely that they will accept the necessary cost reductions that will impact them.

Speaking of costs, Uncle Tony told me about his terrible neighbor, who was always complaining about the cost of things.

I said, "What was he complaining about?"

Uncle Tony said, "Stuff like $1.50 for a coffee, and $3.50 for a sandwich."

I said, "That doesn't sound so outrageous."

Uncle Tony said, "I know. I'm going to stop inviting that guy over for lunch."

Topic 24: Creativity

"Creativity doesn't wait for that perfect moment.
It fashions its own perfect moments out of
ordinary ones."

Source: Bruce Garrabrandt

You absolutely must be creative. That isn't as difficult as it sounds at first. You just need to pay attention to ordinary everyday things and try looking at them in a different way.

For those of you that feel you need techniques to increase creativity, you can research various creativity techniques on the internet. Just be careful someone else doesn't spot your opportunity, while you are playing around with all these techniques. When it comes to creativity, Uncle Tony thought nothing beats looking at something with a fresh set of eyes.

Once when I got a new job, Uncle Tony told me to not let the job description define how I should do my job. He said, "Just look around and see what needs to be done and then do it."

Uncle Tony also thought it didn't hurt if you were a bit of a day dreamer, you just had to be a little careful where you did your day dreaming.

He told me when he was young and working at a minimum wage job, "One of my bosses caught me day dreaming during the morning work assignment meeting."

I asked, "What happened?"

Uncle Tony said, "In front of everyone, my boss asked me if I was paying attention."

I asked, "So, what did you say to your boss?"

Uncle Tony said, "I told him, I'm too poor to pay attention."

Topic 25: Criticism

"Criticism is something we can avoid easily,
by saying nothing, doing nothing,
and being nothing."

Source: Aristotle

Uncle Tony always said, "No matter what you do, someone is going to criticize you for doing it. Get used to it."

If someone tells you they like honest criticism, don't believe them for a moment. Criticism hurts, but don't dwell on it. It is like medicine; it may not taste good, but it is good for you. Your job is to see if you can make good use of the criticism.

The best criticism comes from your enemies. They will tell you the truth about yourself, without any sugar coating. In your heart, you will know whether or not what they said was true. If true, make the necessary changes.

While discussing the topic of criticism, I recall Uncle Tony telling me about a time that a nun criticized him, while he was having a shot of Irish whiskey in a bar.

Uncle Tony replied to the nun, "Who told you that liquor is bad?"

The nun said, "Mother Superior told me."

Uncle Tony said, "Have you ever tried a shot?"

The nun replied, "Never."

Uncle Tony said, "You shouldn't knock something until you have tried it. I'll tell you what, if you drink a shot and tell me you don't like it, I'll stop drinking whiskey."

The nun said, "Okay, but have the bartender put it in a tea cup, so people don't know I am drinking whiskey."

Uncle Tony goes up to the bartender and says, "Give me two shots of Irish whiskey, but put one of them in a tea cup."

The bartender looks at Uncle Tony and says, "Don't tell me that nun is back in here again."

Topic 26: Deadlines

"Deadlines aren't bad.
They help you set priorities.
They make you get going,
when you might not feel like it."

Source: Harvey Mackay

Whenever one of Uncle Tony's crew missed a deadline, he was famous for saying, "Go ahead, tell me how this wasn't your fault."

You should plan to finish your work projects in advance of the deadline and not just fifteen minutes before either. Something always tends to go wrong with every project, so by allowing yourself more time, you can handle these unanticipated challenges and still complete your project on time.

Never start any project without a deadline. Deadlines drive a project; without them, one tends to just wander. Also, you want to schedule key accomplishments at various points so that you can tell early enough whether you need to take corrective action if a project is falling behind. For very complex projects, there are various scheduling software programs available.

If you are responsible for a project and you miss a deadline—it is your fault. Perhaps, you were unrealistic to begin with, didn't set interim goals, or failed to immediately notify those you report to that circumstances had changed, calling for a change in resources or a change in the deadline.

One time Uncle Tony and I were talking about zombies, when he asked me, "What do you call a row of zombies?"

I said, "I don't know."

Uncle Tony said, "A deadline."

Topic 27: Decisions

"Be decisive.
Right or wrong, make a decision.
The road of life is paved with flat squirrels that couldn't
make a decision."

Source: Anonymous

Uncle Tony always thought you are better off making a decision, even if it turns out to be a bad one, than making no decision. Actually, no decision is a decision to do nothing. The impact of indecision is disastrous to your team. They want direction from their leader.

As much as possible, you should seek information and sound advice before reaching a decision. However, as leader, ultimately the decision has to be yours. You should always trust your instincts. You cannot let peer pressure or even data cause you to make a decision that in your heart you know is wrong.

You may want to explain the rationale behind your decision. However, make certain once you have made a decision that no one on your team believes this explanation is an invitation to debate your decision. You must be firmly committed to the decision you have made. Being wishy-washy simply spreads doubt throughout your team and may cause even a good decision to turn out poorly.

Finally, as soon as you realize a decision is a mistake, forget your pride and drop it immediately. If your team knows you can be trusted to drop bad decisions, they will be far more likely to follow your direction even if they have their doubts, since they trust that if you see the direction is clearly wrong, you will swiftly change course.

I recall Uncle Tony telling me that he and his wife had to resist a lot of peer pressure because they decided that they simply did not want children.

Uncle Tony said, "Of course, our children were crying when we left them in the park."

He saw the shocked look on my face and added, "I'm just kidding."

Topic 28: Delegation

"The inability to delegate is one of the biggest problems
I see with managers at all levels."

Source: Eli Broad

As you move from staff and first-line supervision into management, you must force yourself to delegate, perhaps more than you might think appropriate.

Telling others to do things exactly as you would do them isn't a good idea. A new position typically calls for new ways of doing things. Sure, your former approach got you to your new level; but it is unlikely that it will get you to the next level and may even jeopardize your new level.

When it comes to delegation, Uncle Tony expressed the importance of not just telling someone what you want done, but why you need it done. However, Uncle Tony never told anyone how to do something. They know what you want done and why you want it done, so it is up to them to decide how best to get it done.

Uncle Tony told me about a time he was interviewing.

The interviewer asked him, "What is your greatest strength?"

Uncle Tony said, "You tell me."

The interviewer said, "Delegation"

Uncle Tony said, "You are right."

Topic 29: Demotions

"Positivity, confidence, and persistence
are key in life,
so never give up on yourself."

Source: Khalid

Uncle Tony has been down more times than anyone I know. Once during a very difficult time, someone tried to carjack Uncle Tony. They pulled a gun on him and told him to get out of the car.

Uncle Tony said, "Go ahead and shoot."

The carjacker said, "You're crazy," then walked away.

I cannot go into any details about this particular period in Uncle Tony's life, other than to say I think most of us would have said the same thing as Uncle Tony, given all the disappointments he was experiencing at that time.

In spite of his many troubles over the years, Uncle Tony always bounced back. He was certain that everyone else could too. They just needed to become positive, have confidence in themselves, and refuse to give up.

Never assume that a demotion is out of the question for you. Anything can happen in the workplace and sometimes for reasons outside of your control, such as a bad boss.

Your best bet is to remain professional, do what you can to excel in your new lower position, and never hint at any discontent with your new position. Your new position is an opportunity to become more successful this time around.

Your job as a leader is to do everything possible to help anyone in your area who is floundering. Often it takes more than just sending the team member to additional training. Uncle Tony believed that people lived up to what the leader thought of them. If the leader thought highly of their team members, the team members would start thinking more highly of themselves, and their work would reflect their new image. Unfortunately, leaders who think poorly of their team members create their own self-fulfilling prophecy for the team.

If the person still cannot reasonably perform, you need to help them see that they need to change jobs. They probably already know that anyway. Many times people stay in a job they are unsuited for because they have lost their confidence.

I recall hitting a rough patch in life and Uncle Tony tried cheering me up by saying, "Lots of people overcome adversity."

I said, "Name one."

Uncle Tony said, "What about Beethoven? People told him he could never compose music again because he was deaf. Did he listen?"

Topic 30: Details

"If you focus on the smallest details,
you never get the big picture right."

Source: Leroy Hood

Don't get bogged down in the details if you aspire to leadership. You should remember the cliché about not being able to see the forest for all the trees.

However, there is another cliché, which says, "The devil is in the details." So, as you rise up in the organization, you need to find someone to look over the details for you. This person will be the other half of whatever success you achieve, so please treat them accordingly.

Uncle Tony thought clichés were boring and lacked creativity. I asked him what he thought about being detail oriented. He said he wasn't detail oriented, but once came across a guy who was so detail oriented that the guy could tell you the time, place, and location of his death.

I said, "That is impossible, how could that guy know that?"

Uncle Tony said, "A judge told him."

Topic 31: Directions

"Never tell people how to do things.
Tell them what to do,
and they will surprise you with their ingenuity."

Source: Gen. George S. Patton

No one likes a micromanager—at least, no one other than someone who has no idea how to do the job. And even these people will say they don't like a micromanager; but in their hearts they know they need them.

Uncle Tony knows that a lot of you micromanagers don't even realize that you are micromanaging. So here is a clue: If you are talking to one of your team members and you say, "I'm not trying to micromanage…" you might be a micromanager.

When you give direction to a team member, you just want to give the objective and reason. For instance, you say "I need ten copies of this document right away for a noon meeting." Do not say "Go up to the twelfth floor and use the copy machine there to make ten copies of this document." Perhaps your team member knows there is always a long line on the 12th floor to use the copy machine, so the task would take longer following your specific directions.

Of course, you should let them know you are available should they want to run some of their ideas by you. But please make sure they know this isn't an expectation, merely an offer to be there should they need some assistance.

Uncle Tony always thought the best approach was simply to tell his crew what he wanted done and why, then let them decide how best to do it. Often, they would come up with ways to do something that were much different from how Uncle Tony would do it. However, he recognized everyone was different and perhaps their way for them was better than his own way for them. Plus, by letting them decide the "how," he thought this made them more committed to the task.

Uncle Tony never liked having a micromanager for a boss. When one took over an area where he was working, he felt like the boss was always watching him. Eventually, the boss caught Uncle Tony not working.

The boss said, "Tell me why I am not seeing you working."

Uncle Tony replied, "Because I didn't hear you coming."

Topic 32: Education

"Formal education will make you a living;
self-education will make you a fortune."

Source: Jim Rohn

Bill Gates, Steve Jobs, and Mark Zuckerberg never finished college and they made fortunes. What does that teach you? It teaches you that if you are smart, have an innovative idea, and aren't afraid of risk, you could make a fortune. However, they did not accomplish what they did by working their way up the corporate hierarchy.

There are stories of college-educated individuals who seem to lack basic common sense. What does that teach you? Probably nothing, since in all levels of society, we come across individuals who appear to us as lacking common sense.

There is a lot of talk about college graduates buried in student debt and some who are working minimum wage jobs. What does that teach you? If you wish to avoid that fate, you should select your college and your major with an eye toward earning a return on the costs you have invested in your education. In other words, avoid diploma mills and college majors in fields where there is limited demand.

The purpose of this book is to give you some advice on climbing the corporate ladder and achieving some degree of financial success. This may or may not be the path toward your personal happiness. There is a lot of advice out there about the importance of following your dreams. Your education or training, along with the type of work you plan to pursue, are major life-impacting decisions. Uncle Tony advises you to choose carefully, since poverty only wears well on the young.

A formal education and often various professional certifications are a requirement or strongly desired at many organizations. If you don't obtain a degree and possibly various certifications, you will likely have to explain throughout your career why you didn't, if you even get the chance to explain.

Uncle Tony always stressed the importance of getting a good education, perhaps because he knew firsthand how hard it was to get by without a good education. But he always thought common sense was more important than anything.

To illustrate that point, he told me about a tradesman who took his college-educated son camping. That evening the father and son set up their tent and went to sleep.

In the middle of the night, the father wakes his son and says, "Look up at the sky and tell me what you see."

The son says, "I see stars, lots of stars."

The father says, "What does that tell you?"

The son says, "It tells me there are many galaxies, containing suns, with planets like ours revolving around those suns."

The father says, "No silly, it tells you that someone has stolen our tent."

Topic 33: Emotions

"If you do not have control over your mouth,
you will not have control over your future."

Source: Germany Kent

Nothing will cause your undoing, at work or anywhere else, more than the failure to control your emotions. Uncle Tony, who got into his share of fights, used to say, "If you can make your opponent angry, you have increased your chances of winning."

You want to protect your emotional state by avoiding people who are always negative and unhappy, since their attitudes can rub off on you. Another emotional state that can easily rub off on you is a poverty mentality. People with this mentality think and act like they are poor, although they are anything but poor. Keep these people at a distance so that this poverty mentality doesn't rub off on you, since it is difficult to rise in the corporate world if you behave like you are poor.

You want to be sure you associate with positive, upbeat people, who spend within their means, neither underspending nor overspending. Their traits will rub off on you.

Of course, there will be times when you have to express your frustration about work or other things; however, do so in a constructive way by offering alternatives. Unfortunately, there are a rare few times when you have to explode to get your point across regarding how serious the situation is. But please don't use this comment as an excuse for being a loose cannon.

Speaking of controlling one's emotions, Uncle Tony told me, "I like my emotions like my water."

I said, "What do you mean?"

Uncle Tony said, "Bottled, like my water."

Topic 34: Enemies

"The stupid neither forgive nor forget;
the naive forgive and forget;
the wise forgive but do not forget."

Source: Thomas Szasz

There is a saying that if you have no enemies, it means that you aren't doing anything. It is fine to have enemies, since it is impossible to please everyone. If you try, you will only end up disliking yourself. However, you never want to make an enemy if you can avoid it.

Nevertheless, enemies can be useful to you. They can inspire you, as well as be the source of unpleasant truths about yourself and your plans. Friends often cannot bring themselves to tell you your faults, whereas you can count on your enemies to tell you your faults.

In the corporate world, your enemy today could be your partner tomorrow in another situation. Uncle Tony always advised one to treat their enemy no harsher than absolutely necessary and to always provide a path for them to save face. People will judge you as to how you treat your enemies. Therefore, treat them with as much compassion as possible the first time.

Uncle Tony told me that the secret to dealing with enemies is that you need to have patience. Knowing Uncle Tony had some anger management issues, I asked him where his patience came from.

Uncle Tony told me, "Patience is what you have when there are simply too many witnesses around."

Topic 35: Envy

"The truest mark of being born with great qualities,
is being born without envy."

Source: Francois de La Rochefoucauld

Never be envious. Envy is one of the seven deadly sins. Envy makes a person look small. Uncle Tony thought that envy or jealousy was nothing more than a lack of self-confidence, and Uncle Tony was never envious or jealous of anyone.

Perhaps one would not be envious of others if they knew what others gave up to have what they have. Instead, you should see them as an inspiration. They achieved something that you wish to also achieve, so learn from them.

You will find that regardless of your station in life, there will be people envious of you. These people are easy to recognize. They will either tear you down for little things you have done or they will go overboard in pointing out things you could have done better. Avoid the envious; no good can come from associating with them. Uncle Tony thought the same thing with jealous people, a close cousin of envious people.

I recall Uncle Tony telling me his first wife was very jealous.

I asked, "In what way?"

Uncle Tony said, "Every time I just looked at another woman, she would grab the binoculars out of my hands."

Topic 36: Experience

"Good judgment comes from experience
and
experience comes from bad judgment."

Source: Fred Brooks

Experience is a great teacher, even if often a harsh one. Experience is how one develops insight and judgment.

I recall Uncle Tony telling me about a fellow who made a mistake that cost the company $10,000. When the fellow turned in his resignation, to his surprise, the owner of the company refused to accept it. The fellow asked, "Why do you still want me to work for you?"

The owner said, "Because I just invested $10,000 in your experience and I know you aren't going to make that mistake again."

However, you need to evaluate experience. Uncle Tony said, "Often what passes as five years' experience is nothing more than one year of experience repeated five times." He added, "Years with a company should not automatically be thought to represent company loyalty; it may be the result of things that have nothing to do with loyalty." For instance, an employee may lack confidence in their own abilities and so may be reluctant to change jobs.

Although the above focuses on work experience, one should never discount the experiences learned outside of work. Life experiences and work experiences are often interchangeable. You may want to stay open to hiring someone who doesn't have a lot of work experiences but has some unique life experiences that would make them suitable for the position.

Speaking of experiences, Uncle Tony told me about a time that his former wife was depressed because of a serious mistake she had made.

I asked, "What did you do?"

Uncle Tony said, "I told her to treat it as a learning experience and that she should embrace her mistakes."

"Did it work?"

Uncle Tony said, "I guess, she walked up to me and gave me a big hug."

Topic 37: Family

"We think, mistakenly, that success is the result of the
amount of time we put in at work,
instead of the quality of time we put in."

Source: Arianna Huffington

You will hear a lot of talk about work–life balance. The word "balance" means an even distribution. Not putting either family or work ahead of the other. Uncle Tony didn't believe you had to put in long hours at work to make a difference to your organization and crew. He also didn't believe that we have to be so caught up in our family and private life that we can't handle a pressing business problem that comes up during off hours, weekends, or a vacation. He felt it was no different than leaving work to handle a family emergency.

Uncle Tony observed that the most productive work teams are those teams that treat one another as family members. The team as a whole recognizes and celebrates the special events in the lives of each team member. The team is there for individual team members in times of difficulty and covers for them on those occasions when they can't give 100% to their work because of life situations.

Work-life balance means that there are times when work must yield to a personal crisis, and there are other times when personal life must yield to a work crisis.

Uncle Tony used to put in some long hours. One time he was complaining to his wife that he was missing Jimmy's childhood.

His wife replied, "Your son's name is Larry."

Topic 38: Feedback

"I think it's very important to have a feedback loop,
where you're constantly thinking about what you've
done and how you could be doing it better."

Source: Elon Musk

Uncle Tony knew in his daily life that he was benefiting from feedback loops. For instance, the thermostat in his home automatically maintained the desired temperature.

Other feedback loops require your involvement, such as your vehicle's speedometer. The speedometer tells you how fast you are going, and you can either step harder on the accelerator or ease off to get to your desired speed.

Overall, you want to have feedback loops over all the key corporate processes under your responsibility. Doing so will tell you if you are getting the expected results or need to improve the process. Also, be sure you are measuring what is important and not just what is easy to measure.

Just as important, if not more so, is personal feedback. You should give as well as be willing to receive personal feedback. Suggestions for corrective action tend to sting, even when given with the best of intentions—which should always be the reason it is given. Although emphasis is usually on corrective feedback, it is a mistake to neglect reinforcing good performance with feedback.

Uncle Tony was fanatical about giving and receiving feedback.

I recall asking Uncle Tony if being so fanatical about feedback ever got him into trouble.

Uncle Tony said, "Yes, one time I tried to give a sound technician feedback and he got very angry with me. Apparently, sound technicians don't like feedback."

Topic 39: Friends

"Birds of a feather flock together."

Source: William Turner

People will quickly form an opinion of you by observing whom you hang out with. Therefore, choose your friends carefully. Whom we associate with rubs off on us. You want to be sure to hang out with people who are the type of person that you want to be.

After you have wisely selected your friends, stay in contact with them. You should touch base with them every so often and be quick to offer help if you feel they need it. You don't have to wait for them to ask. Typically they will be the type of person reluctant to impose upon you.

I understand that there was more to the above quote from William Turner's book.

"Birds of a feather flock together—until the cat comes."

The above quote reminds us that many of our friends will not stick by us in hard times.

Remember, hard times visit everyone sooner or later. So you must be cautious in selecting your friends and make sure you know the difference between a friend and an acquaintance. When it comes to friends, go for quality rather than quantity.

Uncle Tony told me this story describing a fair-weather friend and the type of friends they tend to attract.

A fair-weather friend came home one morning and told his wife that he spent the night at a friend's home. His suspicious wife called his ten best friends and each said they knew nothing about it.

Uncle Tony then told me what happened one morning when he came home and told his wife that he spent the night at a friend's home.

Knowing how much Uncle Tony liked the ladies, his wife decided to call his ten best friends.

Eight of them confirmed that he had spent the night at their house and two others claimed Uncle Tony was still there.

Make sure you are the type of person who attracts loyal and faithful friends by being that type of person yourself.

Topic 40: Fun

"People rarely succeed
unless they have fun in what they are doing."

Source: Dale Carnegie

Always remember to have fun at work and make sure those around you are also having fun.

If you have seen or read *A Christmas Carol*, remember how old Fezziwig ran his business. Fezziwig was Uncle Tony's role model, and that is how Uncle Tony ran his businesses as well.

Uncle Tony hated walking through a work area where everyone had their head down buried in their work. He thought that there was no sharing of information. He wondered who would want to work in such a dismal place, other than those with no other options.

Uncle Tony told me a story about a time when he started a new job and found out the first day that the boss was a real jerk. The boss gave Uncle Tony an impossible amount of work to get done before the end of the day. As the jerk boss was leaving, he sneered, "Have a nice day." Upon hearing that, Uncle Tony immediately went home. Uncle Tony thought it was a good experience working for a bad boss because they teach you things that you will never do to someone when you become the boss. Just remember to never work very long for a bad boss.

You need to create a workplace where people want to come to work, enjoy their co-workers, and feel appreciated. All workers are volunteers; they volunteer their creativity and energy.

Speaking of fun at work, I remember Uncle Tony telling me about his first week in a new job, and how he got a group of his co-workers to laugh.

I said, "How did you do that?"

"One of my co-workers asked me why I left my last job," said Uncle Tony. "I told him it was something my boss said to me."

One worker asked, "What did your boss say?"

Uncle Tony replied, "She said I was fired."

Topic 41: Generosity

"Generosity is giving more than you can,
and pride is taking less than you need."

Source: Khalil Gibran

You will never regret being generous. If you are insightful, you will likely regret those times when you failed to be generous. Being cheap is demeaning and will result in no one respecting you. Every so often, you should reach for the check. As Uncle Tony would say, "You don't want to get a reputation for having alligator arms."

You especially want to be generous with your team members, both financially and with your time.

You should also extend your generosity to those in slightly higher positions than your own. It never hurts to tactfully invite them to lunch or an after-work outing. But you must only do this from a generosity of spirit, since it is easy to tell if you are doing this just to advance your career.

Speaking of being cheap, Uncle Tony told me about this guy he knew.

The guy told Uncle Tony, "To save money, I'm going to rewire my house instead of hiring an electrician. What do you think of that?"

Uncle Tony said, "I think you are going to be in for a shock."

Topic 42: Goals

"By recording your dreams and goals on paper,
you set in motion the process of becoming the person
you most want to be.

Put your future in good hands—your own."

Source: Mark Victor Hansen

Goals drive everything. If you don't have goals, you are just wandering. Goals allow you to focus. Plus, your staff needs goals that correspond to your goals, and your goals need to correspond to those above you. This approach allows everyone to be working for the good of the organization. And of course everyone needs an action plan stating how they will achieve their goals.

Uncle Tony stressed that your goals need to be short and to the point, so everyone can remember them and recite them off the top of their heads. When it comes to goals, less is more. Remember, you can do anything you wish, you just cannot do everything you wish.

Your goals need to be objectively measurable, specifying quantity, quality, and time periods. They should be a stretch, but not so far that they appear to be unachievable.

You also need to remember that situations change, sometimes dramatically. When that happens, your goals and action plans need to change too. But, this is not an excuse to go without developing goals and action plans. Even if the goals and action plans aren't always helpful in the end, the preparation of them is always going to be helpful since it forces you to think and plan, and not just hope.

Speaking of goals and planning, I asked Uncle Tony, "What are your plans for this weekend?"

Uncle Tony said, "To get some new glasses."

I asked, "Then what?"

Uncle Tony replied, "After that, I'll see."

Topic 43: Gossip

"Strong minds discuss ideas,
average minds discuss events,
weak minds discuss people."

Source: Socrates

Gossip is the constant spreading of personal or private information, whether true or untrue, about another person to others. Uncle Tony said that it doesn't take long for people to figure out that you are a gossip, and if you are talking about others, you will no doubt be also talking about them.

Surely, you can find something more interesting to talk about than someone else's problems. If you find yourself in a situation where you have to talk about someone, be sure all you say are good things about the person.

I can never hear the word "gossip" without remembering this story Uncle Tony told me about four clergymen, who were the best of friends. They were such good friends that they thought it might be helpful to share their personal problems with one another.

The first said, "I often drink to excess." The other three clergymen were shocked.

The second said, "Since you were so honest, I'm going to admit that I have a terrible gambling problem. I've been tempted to take money from the collection plate." Again, the other clergymen were shocked.

The third confessed, "I'm growing very fond of a woman in my church. She is married." Again, the clergymen were shocked.

They all waited for the fourth clergyman to speak. Finally the fourth clergyman broke the silence by saying, "I just don't know how to tell you about my problem."

The remaining three clergymen assured the fourth that his secret would be safe with them.

The fourth clergyman said, "Well, my problem is that I am an incurable gossip."

Topic 44: Greed

"Leadership is a privilege to better the lives of others,
it is not an opportunity to satisfy personal greed."

Source: Mwai Kibaki

Uncle Tony was never greedy. He thought people should share their successes and share their rewards; realize none of it belongs to you, it belongs to all those who helped you achieve whatever you did to receive these tributes.

Make sure your victories are the victories of all those who supported you. If you do that, people will help you be successful or at least not undermine you if they have a jealous nature.

Most important, Uncle Tony insisted that you should do things because you like doing them and not for money.

Greed never turns out well, no matter what. Uncle Tony told this story about a greedy guy who found an old lamp and rubbed it, and then a genie appeared, ready to grant him three wishes.

The greedy guy said, "I'd like a million dollars." As soon as he had made the request of the genie, his bank statement appeared in his hands, showing a recent million-dollar deposit.

Next the greedy guy said, "I want a new Cadillac Escalade." Suddenly, there was one right next to him.

Finally, the greedy guy said, "Make me irresistible to women." Immediately, he turned into a box of chocolates.

Topic 45: Health

"So many people spend their health gaining wealth,
and then have to spend their wealth to regain their
health."

Source: A.J. Materi

Uncle Tony would likely add to the above quote the word *trying*, since once you lose your health, it isn't always possible to regain it.

Do not under any circumstances, neglect your health for work or even for family. Uncle Tony said, "There is a reason the airlines tell you to put the oxygen mask on yourself first. It is because if you can't help yourself, you aren't going to be able to help anyone else."

As for your team members, we all have seen team members who have failed to take care of their health and yet turn in amazing performances. Perhaps, had they maintained their health, they may have been able to accomplish still more or for a longer period in their lives. But that is beside the point; the important thing is to care about your team members and to encourage them to have healthy and long lives.

Speaking of health, Uncle Tony told me a mother once said she was worried about her daughter's strange eating habits. She told him her daughter just lies in bed and only eats yeast and car wax.

Uncle Tony said, "I would not worry too much about her. She will probably rise and shine."

Topic 46: Hiring

"Time spent on hiring
is time well spent."

Source: Robert Half

When it comes to hiring people, you not only need to determine if they have the proper skill sets, but also that they have a good attitude. The proper attitude is as important as the skills. You can teach skills, whereas you will find it is practically impossible to change a person's attitude.

Be extremely leery of applicants who are overly concerned with salary or promotional opportunities. Also please don't neglect your initial gut feeling about an applicant.

And if you aren't sure you have found the right applicant, keep on looking. This is critical: Do not let short-term needs cause you to make a bad long-term decision.

Speaking of hiring, Uncle Tony told me this story about a dog that saw a "Now Hiring" poster in front of a computer store.

The dog took the poster in his mouth and walked into the store and up to the store manager.

The store manager decided to humor the dog, walking him over to a computer. The store manager said, "If you want to work here, you must be able to compose a letter."

The store manager came back and found a perfectly composed letter. The store manager said, "It is also important that you know how to program, so please demonstrate your programming skills."

Later, the store manager returned and found a perfectly running website promoting the store. The store manager said, "Okay, I'm impressed; but, you are still a dog. I can't hire you."

The dog put its paw on the poster where it said, "We are an equal opportunity employer."

The store manager said, "Okay, but another one of the stated qualifications is that you must be bilingual. I know you aren't bilingual."

The dog looked up at the store manager and said, "Meow."

Topic 47: Honesty

"Truth without love is harshness;
it gives us information
but in such a way that we cannot really hear it.
Love without truth is sentimentality,
it supports and affirms us
but keeps us in denial about our flaws."

Source: Timothy Keller

Uncle Tony thought honesty was the best policy, but there were exceptions to every rule—even honesty. Honesty should never be a reason to hurt others, and it isn't necessary to be totally honest in every situation, as the following Uncle Tony story illustrates.

Uncle Tony loved telling this story about an interview.

One of the interviewers asked an applicant what they thought was their greatest weakness.

The applicant replied, "Honesty."

One of the interviewers said, "I don't think honesty is a weakness."

The applicant said, "I don't care what you think."

Topic 48: Ideas

"You can have brilliant ideas,
but if you can't get them across,
your ideas won't get you anywhere."

Source: Lee Iacocca

If you wish to be successful, you need to have ideas. Where do ideas come from? Well, if you are fortunate, they just spring out of you. However, most of us have to develop our ideas. To do so, just look around and try to put dissimilar things together, or look at commonplace things in a new light.

For example, people have been making bread forever. And they have been tearing off a piece of bread with their hands or slicing off a piece of bread with a knife forever. But not until 1928 did a fellow named Otto Rohwedder invent the first functioning single-loaf bread-slicing machine. It wasn't long after people figured out how to wrap and market the sliced bread.

One thing you will have to overcome even when implementing modest ideas is jealousy from peers and possibly even upper management. Another thing you will have to overcome is the professional "devil's advocates." Under the disguise of appearing to want to be helpful, they will always come up with a number of possible reasons why your idea will fail. You may stop believing in your own idea, by the time they get done talking.

Uncle Tony thought these "devil's advocates" don't really want to help you, and the best thing you can do is make sure they aren't in the room when you are presenting your idea. Odds are you already know who they are or can easily find out. They repeat this pattern since they can't come up with ideas of their own.

You also will have to deal with people who have a vested interest in the status quo, along with those who fear any sort of change.

Every idea faces these routine enemies. They can often be defeated by proper preparation and planning and especially by lining up allies in advance of rolling out the idea.

I recall asking Uncle Tony if he had ever come up with any inventive ideas.

Uncle Tony said, "Once I tried inventing a banana-peeling machine."

I asked, "How did that idea turn out?"

He said, "I hoped the idea would bear fruit—but it didn't."

Topic 49: Image

"Change the self image and
you change the personality and the behavior."

Source: Maxwell Maltz

When people at work hear your name, what do you want them to be thinking? That is your image; you need to manage it carefully and have it be consistent.

In addition to your overall demeanor, your appearance is a big part of your image. You need to appear full of energy and looking the part you expect to play in the organization. People sometimes assume that how you take care of yourself is how you will take care of business.

Don't gossip or be around people engaged in gossip—it will reflect back on you. If someone who is not there is being attacked, defend them but be honest in your defense of them.

And no one likes a "topper." You know, the person who always upon hearing of someone else's accomplishment, just has to mention something they have done that's more outstanding.

Be interested in other people, what they are doing, their challenges and their successes. You will find doing so will make others think well of you.

Don't forget that your work environment says a lot about you. Make sure your office or your cubical says what you want it to say. Is it messy, making you look unorganized? Or is it clean and neat, making you look like you are on top of everything?

Speaking of image and clothing, Uncle Tony asked me, "What did the tie say to the hat?"

I said, "I don't know."

"You go on a head, I'll just hang around," said Uncle Tony.

Topic 50: Interview

"Find something you love to do
and you'll never have to work a day in your life."

Source: Undetermined

If you are going on an interview, someone may advise you to figure out the type of person the interviewer wants to hire, and then try to appear as that type of person.

Uncle Tony thought that is bad advice for two reasons. First, if you fool the interviewer into thinking you are someone you are not, you are going to end up having to live a lie. Second, you probably can't keep up the pretense for long before who you really are comes out. Some better advice is to just be yourself. If no one hires you, perhaps you are seeking employment in the wrong line of work or perhaps you need to make some changes in yourself.

When interviewing, you need to know something about the hiring corporation, or if you already work for the corporation, you need to know something about the hiring area. You can demonstrate that knowledge by the questions you ask.

If you are the interviewer, you should prepare your questions in advance and note each candidate's answers. This can help you with your hiring decision.

Uncle Tony always preferred to have a team be part of the interview process, with his voice having no more weight than the others participating. He thought this practice over the years saved him from making some dreadful mistakes. However, he thought you need to be careful whom you place on the hiring team, as some may look at a very qualified applicant as competition rather than someone who can help the team.

Uncle Tony told me his favorite question is to ask the candidate about the last time they got angry at work. Uncle Tony always told them first about the last time that he got angry at work, because he never asked anyone to do anything he would not be willing to do.

You can tell so much from this question. For instance, if they say they have never gotten mad at work, odds are you have an untruthful applicant. Uncle Tony recalled one person who said they got angry at their supervisor because she kept giving them her work to do. Unless the supervisor is asking someone to pick up their cleaning, the supervisor's work is their work.

And finally, you must like the person you are interviewing. If you don't, trust your instincts, and keep looking.

Uncle Tony told me about a time he was being interviewed and was asked where he thought he would be in the company five years from now.

I said, "So what did you say?"

Uncle Tony said, "I think my biggest weakness is not listening."

I said, "That doesn't make sense, you didn't answer the question."

Uncle Tony said, "That's what the interviewer said to me, too."

Topic 51: Leadership

"Outstanding leaders go out of their way to boost the
self-esteem of their personnel.
If people believe in themselves, it's amazing what they
can accomplish."

Source: Sam Walton

If you think your people have to follow your orders because you are the boss, you don't deserve to be boss. You are nothing more than a petty dictator.

There will be times when things don't go well; however, never allow blame to be shifted to any member of your team. The blame rests with you, their leader.

You should never let a day go by without telling as many of your team members as possible how much you appreciate them.

Once while talking about corporate leadership with Uncle Tony, he told me that he had a story for me about a lawyer, a doctor, and a manager. He told me the three were discussing which was better, having a wife or a girlfriend.

The lawyer said, "The girlfriend is best. If you find you and your wife can't get along, you end up in a costly divorce."

The doctor said, "No, the wife is best. It is a proven fact that married men live longer than single men."

The manager said, "You are both wrong. It is best to have both a wife and a girlfriend."

The lawyer and doctor both asked, "Why do you say that?"

The manager says, "When the wife thinks you are with your girlfriend, and your girlfriend thinks you are with your wife, you can go to the office and get some work done."

Topic 52: Listening

"We have two ears and one mouth
so that we can listen twice as much as we speak."

Source: Epictetus

Remember, you aren't learning when you are the one doing the talking. You learn by listening. And the more you listen, the more you will be perceived as a good conversationalist. Uncle Tony told me that one of his ex-wives told him that he wasn't a very good listener. Uncle Tony added, "At least I think that was what she said."

Honest listening is a difficult skill to learn. Usually, instead of listening, we are thinking what we are going to say as soon as the current speaker stops for a breath of air. The more you practice, the better listener you will become. And always stay on guard to avoid falling back into bad habits.

There are many things you can do to show you are listening, such as nodding, restating what you have heard, and asking clarification as to what you have heard.

You should also listen for what isn't being said, which at times can be more important than what is being said. You should pay attention to your gut instincts as well as the speaker's body language. Also, if you know much about the speaker, at times you may suspect they are leaving out details that would contradict their position. At such times, you can tactfully ask questions to draw out the missing information.

Speaking of listening, I remember one time Uncle Tony was telling me about a problem he was having, when he added, "It is times like this, when I wish I had listened to my uncle."

I asked Uncle Tony, "What did he say?"

Uncle Tony replied, "I don't know, I wasn't listening."

Topic 53: Loyalty

"If you're not loyal to your team, you can get by for
a while; but, eventually you will need to rely on their
loyalty to you, and it just won't be there."

Source: Tim Schafer

Whether you are working for someone or someone is working for you, loyalty is the number one criterion. One can forgive a lot of things, but not disloyalty. However, loyalty is a two-way street. Of course your team members should be loyal to you and not undermine your leadership, but as a leader, you owe loyalty to your team members. When it comes to their mistakes, realize we all make them. You will find they will do the same for you.

If you find yourself in a situation where you cannot bring yourself to be loyal to the person you report to, for the sake of your own mental health, you need to find another position. Until you do, the only honorable thing for you to do is not be disruptive. Hopefully, you can find another position somewhere else in the corporation. If not, you must leave the corporation. Did you put away your "I quit" money? Without such a fund, you can never be honorable under all circumstances.

When it comes to those who report to you, you must respect them, appreciate them, and carry them over rough spots in their lives. Even if you do these things and more, you will sometimes have a disloyal or even hostile team member. There will be disagreements between you and team members; this is natural and often helpful. These areas of disagreement can often be resolved with a face-to-face talk or the presentation of additional information. These situations have nothing to do with disloyalty. Disloyalty is when there is a pattern of behavior that clearly demonstrates their dislike for you.

As for dealing with a hostile team member, never be any harsher than absolutely necessary. How you treat your enemies says a lot about you to others. With that said, know that every moment you delay in getting rid of this person, the more you put yourself at risk.

Speaking of loyalty, I recall this story that Uncle Tony told me about a German shepherd, a Doberman, and a cat who all die and go to heaven. God asks the German shepherd what he believes in.

The German shepherd says, "Loyalty to my master and discipline."

God says, "That is good and you may sit on my right."

God turns towards the Doberman and asks the same question.

The Doberman says, "I believe in loyalty to my master and protecting my master."

God says, "That is also good and you may sit on my left.

Next God turns towards the cat and again asks the same question.

The cat says, "I believe you are in my seat."

Topic 54: Lunch

"Once a month go to lunch
with someone who knows more about your business
than you do."

Source: H. Jackson Brown

Lunch is an opportunity to learn something from someone more successful than yourself or someone more accomplished in some area that you would like to know more about. Always remember that who you are having lunch with is far more important than what you are eating or where you are having lunch. As for how you should act at one of these lunches, follow Uncle Tony's advice. You have two ears and one mouth; use them in that proportion.

It is nice to have lunch with your friends, but at least once a month do your best to have lunch with someone who can help you in your career. If the party you are having lunch with is more successful than you are, pick up the check if at all possible. The other party will likely insist they pay, but you can counter that offer by saying perhaps they can pay next time. This has the advantage of there possibly being another lunch with this person.

If you are fortunate enough to be having drinks after work with a group of people who are at a higher corporate level than you, make sure you pick up the tab for a round of drinks. Doing so will earn their respect and if they aren't too many levels above, perhaps you may even be viewed as a peer.

Speaking of business lunches, Uncle Tony told me about a time that he was having lunch with a fellow who was in the same line of work.

Uncle Tony said, "We were having a tug-of-war over the check and my hand slipped and I accidently knocked the rest of the other fellow's lunch all over him."

I asked, "What happened?"

Uncle Tony said, "I told him it looks like lunch is on you."

Topic 55: Mentor

"The mind is not a vessel to be filled,
but a fire to be kindled."

Source: Plutarch

Uncle Tony's first rule of mentoring is that the person you are considering mentoring must be worth the effort. If you aren't certain, don't build up the hopes of someone who doesn't have what it takes to climb the corporate ladder. However, it is not your job to dash anyone's hopes. You must always be respectful of someone seeking your advice. It is a great compliment. However, when giving that advice, you must be totally honest, yet tactful.

Without even knowing it, you may be someone's mentor simply by your daily actions.

The flip side of the coin is finding someone to mentor you. Don't approach someone asking if they will mentor you. You need to be much more tactful. A better approach is to simply exchange pleasantries with the person frequently. As time goes on, it would be natural for you to ask this person's opinion on something.

If the potential mentor's recommendations seem reasonable, give them a try. If they do not seem reasonable to you, don't disagree. Instead, ask some "what if" questions to gain a better understanding of the advice. Perhaps you will feel more comfortable with that advice.

You can be successful without a mentor, especially if you adopt the behaviors of those you found successful. But it helps if you have a mentor who can bring you to the attention of other executives as a rising star.

While talking about mentoring, Uncle Tony told me there was a kidnapping once where he worked.

I asked, "What does that have to do with mentoring?"

Uncle Tony said, "I was mentoring a young student intern."

I said, "Okay, so?"

Uncle Tony said, "Well, I caught him napping."

Topic 56: Morale

"The mind is its own place,
and in itself can make a heaven of hell,
a hell of heaven."

Source: John Milton

Regardless of your position in a corporation, make yourself responsible for everyone's morale, from the lowest employee to the highest. No matter how high in the organization one is, they can usually use a boost in their morale. They will remember the person who provided that boost.

Never neglect the morale of those far below you on the corporate organization chart. They need to feel that what they are doing is important and matters. Believe me, you will not regret winning their hearts.

As for your peers or competition, the same goes for them. You should help them and make them feel good about themselves. One day, they may even applaud your promotion.

You may be surprised to learn that even those far higher on the corporate organization chart than you appreciate a compliment.

Uncle Tony was telling me how important high morale was to any organization. He thought it was so important that he went to a consultant to get some tips on how to boost his crew's morale.

I asked him, "How did that turn out?"

Uncle Tony replied, "It started out okay, with the consultant telling me whatever I came up with to boost morale, I should not come across at being too clever, witty, or even charming."

I said, "That sounds okay."

Uncle Tony said, "After the consultant said that, it went downhill."

I said, "Why do you say that?"

Uncle Tony said, "Next, the consultant suggested I just be myself."

Topic 57: Motivation

"Motivation is the art of getting people
to do what you want them to do
because they want to do it."

Source: Dwight D. Eisenhower

There has been plenty written about motivation tools and various hierarchies of needs that can be used to motivate team members. No doubt they probably work to some degree. However, if you conduct yourself in a manner that earns your team's respect, pay attention to them, appreciate them, and encourage them to believe in themselves, that will result in long-run motivation.

Uncle Tony always believed in seeing the best in his crew. He would downplay their weaknesses and play up their strengths just enough, but never so much that they didn't believe his assessment of them. He never found anyone that did not more than live up to his high opinion of them.

He stressed when you compliment someone on something they are doing, be sure to be very specific. Team members are good at detecting empty praise.

For example, Uncle Tony told me that his first wife once said to him, "I feel like I look fat. I need you to give me a compliment."

Uncle Tony said, "Sure. You have excellent eyesight."

Topic 58: Names

"A name represents identity,
a deep feeling and holds tremendous significance
to its owner."

Source: Rachel Ingber

Uncle Tony thought you could get so much mileage out of remembering and using people's names. Don't tell yourself that you aren't good at remembering names. No one is, until they make a sincere effort to do so. There are all kinds of techniques suggested for remembering names, so look into them and try to find a couple that will work for you.

The important point to take away is that you should remember and use people's names, if you want to increase your chances of being successful.

Uncle Tony told me, "Always remember the sweetest word in the English language to most people is their own name."

I said, "Why did you say most people and not everyone?"

Uncle Tony replied, "Well, to me the sweetest words in the English language are 'not guilty.'"

Topic 59: Negotiations

"Always go into meetings or negotiations
with a positive attitude.
Tell yourself you're going to make this the best deal
for all parties."

Source: Natalie Massenet

When it comes to negotiations, the one who is willing or able to walk away is the one with the power. This is true whether you are negotiating a major contract or in more personal day-to-day negotiations.

When in a negotiation, remember that there are usually only a few points that actually matter. This is true for both major contracts and personal day-to-day negotiations.

One technique taught in negotiation training is to start with a list of sham requirements and act as if they are important to you. These points should be unreasonable to the other party or be extremely costly to them. Otherwise, the other party can accept without hurt and gain credit for being flexible. Toward the end of the negotiation, you can concede these points in exchange for a fair share of the more important points.

Uncle Tony felt uncomfortable using the above technique for personal or team member negotiations, which made him reluctant to endorse such an approach for major contract negotiations. Still, you should be aware of it.

One should always keep in mind that often 80% of concessions will take place in the last 20% of the negotiations, so don't be impatient.

Before one goes into any negotiation, they need to be prepared. Being prepared is knowing what is your non-negotiable position. If possible, one should have a support team or some method of accessing supporting information quickly. Plus, it helps if you can think fast, as this Uncle Tony story illustrates.

Uncle Tony sometimes worked as a union negotiator. One time he was negotiating a sick time provision with a company, when the company's human resource director held up the sports page of the daily paper and said, "This man called in sick yesterday and the paper shows that yesterday he won a local golf tournament."

Uncle Tony said, "Wow, he won although he was sick."

Topic 60: Networking

"You can have everything in life that you want,
if you will just help enough other people
get what they want."

Source: Zig Ziglar

How many times have you heard the phrase, "It's not what you know, it is who you know." Uncle Tony thought the reason you keep hearing this phrase is because it is true. You should make it your mission to get to know people who can influence your career for the better. And the best way to get to know the people who can help you is to do something for them, regardless of how small a service you can provide.

Make sure you stay in touch with those most important to your success. Be sure to remember the 80/20 rule. This rule says that 80% of the value you derive from your contacts will come from 20% of your contacts. So, for this important 20%, make sure you devote 80% of your contact time to these people.

If you are not comfortable talking to someone, it is unlikely that you will build a strong relationship with that individual. Ask someone a level or maybe two above you to lunch and pick up the tab. These networking lunches are to your benefit.

Don't hide your accomplishments, but it is a good idea to be more interested in the accomplishments of those who can help your career. If you make it clear you admire their accomplishments, hard work, and intelligence, they will start thinking you are pretty smart to recognize these traits in them.

If you hang around disgruntled employees or those who see the worse in everything, it will not help you.

Uncle Tony had a story for everything, and networking is no exception.

Uncle Tony called his wife saying, "Some of the top people in the organization just invited me to a fishing trip this weekend. They are leaving this evening. I don't have time to get home and get ready, so could you pack me a couple pairs of jeans, T-shirts, and pajamas? Also, I need my fishing rod and tackle box."

Uncle Tony came home to pick up his suitcase, fishing rod, and tackle box, saying to his wife, "Are you sure you packed everything?"

His wife said, "I'm certain I did."

When Uncle Tony returned Sunday night, he said, "Hey, you forgot to pack my pajamas."

His wife replied, "No I didn't, I put them in your tackle box!"

Topic 61: No

"Real freedom is saying 'no'
without giving a reason."

Source: Amit Kalantri

Saying no is so hard for so many people, but if you are going to be successful, you must learn to say this word: "No." You will find the more you say no, the easier it becomes. Plus, it prevents you from making promises that you can't keep.

Not only is saying no the greatest time management tool there is, but it will make you more successful. Saying no will free up time to allow you to focus on what matters to your success, such as saying yes to requests from one's boss.

Besides, you can always change your mind and say yes later. Often you will find the requester's appreciation is greater than had you immediately said yes. If the requester has already found someone to take on the task, well so much the better for you.

Remember you are not required to give a reason. Besides, the person who is asking you to do something is unlikely to accept your reasons for saying no; so you find yourself in a pointless debate and possibly even more likely of making an enemy than with the simple no answer. If you do offer a reason, perhaps give a vague one like "I have another project I need to work on" or something similar to that.

Uncle Tony rarely gave an excuse for saying no, but when he did, he would simply say, "I need to spend more time with my bartender."

Topic 62: Now

"Do it now.
Sometimes 'later' becomes 'never.'"

Source: Unknown

The time to do anything is right now. Uncle Tony thought odds are if you tell yourself you will get to it later, you probably will not.

If for some reason you can't handle a request at that moment, you should let the person know when you might be able to get to it.

Uncle Tony knew he had a problem with putting things off. In fact, he told me he bought a book about how to stop procrastinating.

I asked, "Did the book help?"

Uncle Tony said, "I never got around to reading it."

Topic 63: Office

"The way your desk looks
gives away an awful lot of information
about your inner life."

Source: Lily Bernheimer

Don't be the person who insists upon a larger office, because it will just make you look small. The key words are "insists upon." What you want is big responsibilities, and if that comes with a big office, that is fine. If it doesn't come with a big office, that is also fine.

Uncle Tony thought that you should always try to be located somewhere in the vicinity of those who report to you. That way, you will be more available to them, plus you will know each of them much better than if you were in some distant location.

You should keep in mind that your office or your cube or whatever is a reflection of you. People will judge you based in part on what your work area looks like. Just make sure it reflects the person that you want to present to others.

If at all possible, try to make use of a round table in your office, rather than a desk. This tends to reduce the status differences among those at the table, which encourages freer communications.

Uncle Tony asked me, "Are you familiar with the legend of King Arthur and his knights sitting in front of his big huge desk?"

I just looked puzzled.

Uncle Tony said, "No? Well, neither am I. But I have a hunch you have heard of King Arthur and his Knights of the Round Table."

Topic 64: Paper

"Paper clutter is nothing more than
postponed decisions."

Source: Barbara Hemphill

Uncle Tony said that victory belongs to the swift, so please avoid burying yourself in paper. It will smother you. Think hard whether or not you need to file something. Paper, in all its forms, just slows you down. If you need something, go back to the originating area and get it from them. However, if it is something critical, you may want to keep it. The originating area, for various reasons, may no longer have the document.

Also, it is a good idea to date any document you file and date it again every time you use it. This will tell you how necessary the document is when you are going through your files. Any search through files is an opportunity to purge your files, and you will find that the majority of your files are unnecessary.

I'm guessing some of you are waiting for an Uncle Tony joke. I recall once asking Uncle Tony if he knew any jokes about paper.

Uncle Tony said, "I don't tell jokes about paper. Paper jokes are tearable."

Topic 65: Passion

"There is no passion to be found in playing small,
in settling for a life
that is less than the one you are capable of living."

Source: Nelson Mandela

Uncle Tony thought that if you are just going through the motions, you are never going to get anywhere. You need passion for what you are doing, or you should find something else to do.

I remember hearing a story about a young man, who approached Uncle Tony asking for knowledge.

Uncle Tony took the young man to the sea, waded in with him, and then dunked him in the water. As he let the young man up, Uncle Tony asked the young man, "What do you want?"

The young man said, "Knowledge."

Uncle Tony held him under the water longer this time. Letting him up, Uncle Tony said, "What do you want?"

The young man replied, "Knowledge."

Uncle Tony repeated the process a number of times.

Eventually the young man replied, "I want air."

Uncle Tony said, "Good, now when you want knowledge as much as you wanted air, you shall have it."

I thought this was something Uncle Tony did, but so much time has passed that I am no longer sure. Maybe Uncle Tony just helped Socrates hold the young man under water.

Topic 66: Perfection

"The pursuit of excellence is gratifying and healthy.
The pursuit of perfection is frustrating, neurotic and a
terrible waste of time."

Source: Edwin Bliss

If you are struggling with the difference between perfection and excellence, the 80/20 rule may help you. The rule says that 80% of your outcomes result from 20% of your inputs. In most cases, pursuing that additional 20% of outcome to reach 100% of perfection is simply not worth the effort if it is even attainable.

Usually, there is nothing more irritating or time wasting than a perfectionist. Even striving for that last little 5% or 10% in hopes of achieving perfection is too costly to be practical. Plus, most of what we do in life and certainly in the corporate world is simply not that critical.

Don't be a perfectionist and don't allow them a say in your operations. They are usually more trouble than they are worth.

I recall asking Uncle Tony, "Is it true that humans are incapable of perfection?"

Uncle Tony replied, "The closest a human ever comes to perfection is when they are completing a job application.

Topic 67: Persistence

"Nothing in this world can take the place of persistence.

Talent will not: nothing is more common than
unsuccessful men with talent.

Genius will not: unrewarded genius is almost a proverb.

Education will not: the world is full of educated der-
elicts.

Persistence and determination alone are omnipotent."

Source: Calvin Coolidge

President Calvin Coolidge covered this topic. So in the words of
Uncle Tony, "You will be surprised at what you can accomplish if you
simply do not give up."

I recall talking to Uncle Tony about the importance of persistence.
During our conversation, Uncle Tony told me this story about a young
student who was away at college.

As the young student was having lunch at a little restaurant, he
opened a letter from his mom. In the letter was a twenty-dollar bill.

As much as the student could use the twenty dollars, he remem-
bered a shabbily dressed character who was always just standing on the
corner by the restaurant. He decided he was going to do a good deed,
so he wrapped the twenty-dollar bill in a napkin and wrote, "PERSIS-

TENCE!" on the napkin. As he walked past the character, he handed the fellow the napkin.

A few days later, the student again was having lunch at the restaurant. The same fellow to whom he had given the twenty dollars enclosed in a napkin tapped him on the shoulder. The man handed the student five twenty-dollar bills.

The student said, "What is this for?"

The man replied, "Persistence came in first in the second race at the track the other day."

Topic 68: Planning

"In preparing for battle
I have always found that plans are useless,
but planning is indispensable."

Source: Dwight D. Eisenhower

Uncle Tony believed there is a lot of truth in the cliché: "Fail to plan, plan to fail." However, somewhat along the lines of President Eisenhower, he preferred the annual plan to even five-year plans or those ridiculously longer plans. With the annual plan, at the end of the year you can assess where you are at, where you want to be next year, and how you are going to get there. That is not to say you shouldn't have a general idea of where you want to be at in five, ten, or more years. Just that you should not invest a lot of effort in developing specifics that go far into the future, since the world changes, often rather quickly.

Always remember that plans are just guidelines, not straightjackets. If a great opportunity comes up, take it even if it isn't in your plan.

You don't need to start out with extremely detailed plans and if you do, most likely such an approach will stop you from planning. Just start with a general plan and as time goes on and you learn more, you can make it more specific. The important thing is that you have a plan. If you have not put your plan into writing, it is just a wish.

Keeping your plan to just a few key objectives and monitoring your progress weekly alerts you to the need to take corrective action so that you will achieve your objective.

Avoid impossible time frames, which do nothing but discourage. Keep your plan realistic and attainable with continuous effort on your part.

Every day, look at your plan and ask yourself what is the most important thing you can do for yourself, your bosses, and your team that you serve.

Uncle Tony always considered planning important; but I was surprised at how obsessed he was with vacation planning.

So one day I asked him, "Why are you so obsessed over vacation planning?"

Uncle Tony said, "It is because of my first marriage. During my first marriage, I went on vacation to the Smoky Mountains. Guess what?"

I said, "No idea."

Uncle Tony said, "My wife got pregnant. The next year, I went on vacation to the Grand Canyon. Guess what?"

I said, "Don't tell me that she got pregnant again."

Uncle Tony said, "Yep, and the following year I went on vacation to Yellowstone Park. And would you believe it, she got pregnant again."

I asked, "What happened the next year when you went on vacation?"

Uncle Tony replied, "The next year I decided to take my wife on vacation with me."

Topic 69: Power

"Nearly all [people] can stand adversity,
but if you want to test a [person's] character,
give [them] power."

Source: Abraham Lincoln

Power will permit you to do a lot of good or a lot of harm. Uncle Tony believed that you should always use it wisely for good, rather than merely to enrich yourself.

Be careful of the power you acquire. Power will corrupt your character unless you are vigilant. The Romans were so wary of power that when they granted one of their successful generals a "Triumph," they always had someone stand behind the general during the ceremony, continuously whispering, "Remember, you are a mortal!"

Funny thing about "power," the more you give it up, the more you have. This isn't intuitive, and it may not make sense at first glance, but it is true.

Just be careful who you give it up to and never let it concentrate in the hands of a person or a couple of people.

And always remember what Uncle Tony said: "With great power comes a great electric bill."

Topic 70: Preparation

"By failing to prepare, you are preparing to fail."

Source: Benjamin Franklin

You should always be prepared for significant things you have to do. Uncle Tony thought just a little advance preparation will make your life so much smoother and probably more successful.

As an example, suppose you have to drive to an important meeting tomorrow. You should know the route, and your vehicle should be gassed and ready to take you there. You need to make sure your clothing is ready—no missing buttons or stains. You may want to have some small bills, should there be valet parking. Of course, there are many other things you need to do in order to be prepared for an important meeting, but this will give you an idea of what it means to be prepared.

Another example is when giving a speech. You should practice and practice until you feel totally confident. You need to arrive early so you can get comfortable with the facility, and perhaps strike up a conversation with some of the early arrivals.

After each event or situation, if something came up that you weren't prepared for and that you are likely to experience again, make a note to add that to your preparation.

Uncle Tony was a believer in being prepared. His first wedding was an example of his attention to being prepared.

The priest said to Uncle Tony, "You may now read the vows you have prepared."

Uncle Tony just stood there and finally said, "I think I may have misunderstood your instructions last week."

The priest said, "Just read what you wrote."

Uncle Tony sheepishly said, "Okay. A, E, I, O, U."

Topic 71: Priorities

"The key is not to prioritize what's on your schedule,
but to schedule your priorities."

Source: Stephen Covey

It is a fact of life that not everything you or your team does has the same return on the investment of your time and energy. Uncle Tony was always good about dropping low-value activities to make time for what was important to him.

Of course, when it comes to your boss's priorities, they are your priorities. You should only tactfully question them if you believe doing so would be in the best interest of your boss.

Think about all the low-value activities you perform, which keep you from doing something important. Ask yourself, are you simply caught up in trivialities? Other times, we use low-value activities to put off doing something difficult but important.

You need to put first things first. The minor stuff you can delegate, hire out, or simply leave undone.

Here is a story that Uncle Tony used to tell about a teacher who was trying to teach her students about priorities.

The teacher filled a jar with rocks and asked her students, "Is the jar full?"

The students replied, "Yes."

The teacher then poured some small pebbles into the jar, while giving the jar a shake every so often to ensure the pebbles filled the space around the rocks. She again asked the students, "Now, is the jar full?"

Again, they said, "Yes."

This time the teacher poured sand into the jar, again giving it a shake every so often so that the sand filled all the empty spaces in the jar.

The teacher explained that the important things were the rocks, the things that you could not do without. The pebbles are things that matter, but somehow you could get along without them. The sand is everything else. She went on to say, had she put the sand in the jar first, there would have been no room for the things that mattered. So, you need to prioritize the things that are critical to you.

Uncle Tony told me that he thought this was a beautiful story, yet he was glad he wasn't there.

I asked him, "Why is that?"

Uncle Tony said, "I bet I could have poured some beer into that jar."

I replied, "I guess you could have, but what would that have proved?"

Uncle Tony said, "That no matter how full you are, there is always room for a beer."

Topic 72: Promises

"The best way to keep one's word
is to not give it."

Source: Napoleon Bonaparte

Uncle Tony also was a believer in the best way to keep your word is to not give it. However, he knew there are times when you must make a commitment. In those situations, you must be absolutely faithful in keeping that promise. Even the slightest failure to keep any promise, even a minor one, will harm your reputation. People must be able to absolutely trust your word.

Speaking of promises, Uncle Tony told me about a time he was in court and there was a jury-tampering trial going on.

The prosecuting attorney said to the witness, "Isn't it true you promised to undermine this case for $10,000?"

The witness did not respond.

The prosecuting attorney in a louder voice said, "Again, isn't it true you promised to undermine this case for $10,000?"

Again, the witness did not respond.

The judge turned to the witness and said, "You have to answer the question."

"Oh," the surprised witness said to the judge, "I thought he was talking to you."

Topic 73: Promotions

"Opportunities don't happen,
you create them."

Source: Stephen Covey

The purpose of this book is to help you rise to middle management in the corporate world. Once in middle management, you may decide to try to make it to the executive ranks. Just remember, the higher you rise in the hierarchy, the more you will have to work through others and the further away you will be from the actual work. So, if you enjoy the "doing" part of work, you need to think about how high you wish to rise.

Uncle Tony knew that if you want a promotion, it takes more than just doing your job well. You need to find a way to showcase your skills without antagonizing your peers. You should always be willing to help others and you may become the problem solver in your area for your teammates. No doubt, you can find other ways to tactfully stand out. You need to do all this without getting a reputation for working long hours and weekends; otherwise, management may come to believe you cannot handle additional responsibilities. Never forget, it is important that you get to know people who will be willing to advance your career.

Some of you may be aware of "The Peter Principle," which says there is a tendency for people to get promoted up to the level of their incompetence. It seems to come from a desire to reward people for a job they are doing well. The problem is that although they are doing their current job well, they may not have the skills to be successful in the next rung up the corporate ladder.

Promoting technical people into supervisory positions calls for considerable care. Some may excel, since they know the work so well and can assist people; but others simply may not have the leadership skills and will have a difficult time relating to people or will micromanage them.

If you are responsible for technical people, you have to find ways, like special training, to reward these people who perform their jobs well but either don't possess the skills for the next level or have no desire to leave their current level since they enjoy the work so much.

Speaking of promotions, Uncle Tony told me years ago he was offered a promotion by a Canadian firm.

I said, "What happened?"

Uncle Tony said, "My boss told me that they were promoting me to an entry-level management position in some little town in Canada."

I said, "Well, did you take the job?"

Uncle Tony said, "It didn't exactly work out. I told my boss, there was nothing in that town but bar girls and hockey players. I could tell my boss was mad when he said that his mother was from that town."

I said, "So what did you do then?"

Uncle Tony said, "I asked him what team she was on."

Topic 74: Punctuality

"If you aren't 15 minutes early, you're late."

Source: U.S.M.C.

Uncle Tony always thought being on time for even the smallest of events communicates that you are a person who takes time commitments seriously. If someone is considering you to be in charge of a project, they will likely take note of your punctuality.

Plus, often by arriving early, you can find many advantages that a late arriver will miss out on, such as better seating.

Uncle Tony once told me a story involving being late. He said, "As I was driving down this country road, I saw a guy holding up a sign. The sign said, 'The end is near! Turn around before it is too late!'"

I asked, "What did you do?"

Uncle Tony said, "Nothing, I just thought the guy was one of those religious zealots."

I said, "So?"

Uncle Tony said, "I just wish that sign would have said, 'Bridge out.'"

Topic 75: Quality

"Strive for progress,
not perfection."

Source: David Perlmutter

Uncle Tony always insisted that whatever you do—your work, your relationships, your clothing, your vehicle, your office décor, etc.—do it with quality.

It doesn't always have to be 100% top quality. In some situations, it should not be 100% because the difference in cost between the highest quality and the acceptable level of quality just below the highest is usually huge. Often, your goal is good quality, but not the absolute best or something that is barely okay.

I knew Uncle Tony had many different jobs, so one day I asked him, "I know you have done about every job there is over the years. Was there any job that you wanted to do but never got the chance?"

Uncle Tony said, "Well, I always wanted to be quality inspector at a mirror company."

I said, "Why?"

Uncle Tony said, "I could just see myself doing that job."

Topic 76: Recognition

"Don't work for recognition,
but do work worthy of recognition."

Source: H. Jackson Brown, Jr.

When we enter the realm of individual awards, we are on exceedingly dangerous ground. Given out too freely, they become meaningless at best. And if given out for the wrong reason or to the wrong person, they become a source of resentment.

In most organizations, the 80/20 rule prevails, in that 20% of your team will receive 80% of the rewards. I hope this isn't true, as this situation looks like you are playing favorites. What is more likely is that whenever a challenging task surfaces, you tend to go back to the same people who in the past have successfully met challenging tasks.

Here is Uncle Tony's solution to the appearance of unfairness in the distribution of recognition awards. Keep a list of all your team members. Make sure each time a challenging task surfaces, which will likely result in an award if handled competently, you go to a person on your list who hasn't been asked before. Of course, it has to be someone who is reasonably qualified. Some will turn down the opportunity, but at least you offered. The idea is that over a period of time, everyone will have had an opportunity to volunteer for a task that will result in an award if completed successfully.

Celebrating team victories as much as possible builds group cohesion and reduces the possibility of jealousy about team members.

If you have a reputation for good work, are willing to volunteer just to be helpful, and identify problems and solutions to those problems, you are likely to receive considerable recognition.

I asked Uncle Tony, "Did you ever receive any awards or some sort of recognition at all the different jobs you have had over the years?"

Uncle Tony said, "Once, I came close."

I said, "What do you mean?"

Uncle Tony said, "Well once, I walked away with an 'Employee of the Month' award. However, security stopped me as I was leaving the building."

Topic 77: Reputation

"You can't build a reputation on what you are going
to do."

Source: Henry Ford

You must guard and defend your reputation at all times, since it is so important for your success. You want a reputation of honesty, intelligence, and reliability. Don't forget your social media accounts, since it is likely your current and future employers will be checking. Do your social media accounts reflect well upon you?

Hopefully, no one will ever ask you to do something that you know is seriously wrong. If you do it, not only will you lose your own self-respect; but also, you will lose the respect of everyone else. And if no one respects you, no one is going to trust you with greater responsibilities.

Therefore, Uncle Tony said that you must put away some "I Quit Money." If you have it, most likely you will not have to use it. If you don't have it, you will wish for the rest of your life that you did.

Most importantly, you create your reputation with your acts far more than with your words. Uncle Tony always said, "If someone is constantly mentioning their integrity or other positive trait, it is likely they are lacking that trait; otherwise, they would not feel the need to mention it so frequently."

Uncle Tony told me one of his experiences concerning reputations.

When he was young, he went to confession and told the priest, "Bless me father for I have sinned by being with a loose girl."

The priest said, "Is that you, Tony?"

Tony said, "Yes father, it is."

The priest said, "What girl were you with?"

Tony said, "I'm sorry, father I cannot tell. I don't want to ruin her reputation."

The priest said, "It wasn't that Carla Ricci, was it?"

Tony said, "I cannot say."

The priest said, "Perhaps it was Gina Bollo? Or was it Concetta D'Agostino?

Tony said, "I cannot name the girl."

The priest persisted, "Tell me, was it Rosa Palma?"

Tony said, "I will never tell."

The frustrated priest said, "Okay, you did well not telling. Still, you must atone. For the next month you cannot be an altar boy."

Tony's buddy was waiting for him outside and asked, "What happened?"

Tony said, "I got a month's vacation and the names of four girls I want to meet."

Topic 78: Resignation

"You can't blame someone for leaving,
if you never gave them a reason to stay."

Source: Unknown

There are any number of reasons that could result in you resigning your position. The most likely one is you ending up reporting to a boss that you simply cannot stand. If you have made a sincere effort to get along with this person and it is still not working, you need to find another position inside or outside of your company.

Uncle Tony knew that it is always easier to find a position in another company if you currently have a job. So don't quit your current job until you have another.

When you find another position, always remember to give at least two weeks notice to your current employer. However, any more than that is not only unnecessary, but it is unlikely you will be treated the same as before you gave your resignation.

It is a good idea to write your ex-boss a thank you letter under almost all circumstances. If you are leaving under difficult circumstances, still try to find something during your time of employment for which you can express sincere appreciation. If your current employer conducts exit interviews to find out why you are leaving, please remember the words of Uncle Tony, "Don't burn your bridges behind you as you leave."

Uncle Tony knew a lot about quitting jobs. Once he told me he had quit a job as a taxi driver.

I asked him, "Why?"

He said, "Because people were always talking behind my back."

Topic 79: Resources

"The greatest asset of a company
is its people."

Source: Jorge Paulo Lemann

People are a corporation's most important resource. Uncle Tony thought most corporations say this; some of them actually believe it. Of those who believe it, some actually act like it. When you eventually have people reporting to you, know they are your most important resource and act in such a way that your team knows that you consider them important.

All resources are precious, especially your human resources. Make sure you avoid the common practice of allocating too many resources to unimportant activities and too few to important activities. Uncle Tony said, "The question isn't is this worth doing, but is this the best use of my resources."

Strange as it may seem, you are probably better off being short on resources to get the job done than you are with having way more than you need. Being short on resources forces you to be creative, whereas too many resources tend to make you a bit too casual.

Regarding a shortage of resources, here is an Uncle Tony story you may like.

One day Uncle Tony met one of his associates that owned a business. Uncle Tony said, "You look down, what is the matter?"

The business associate said, "I need some cash for my business and I have no idea where I am going to get it."

Uncle Tony said, "I'm glad to hear that. For a moment, I was afraid you might try to borrow the money from me."

Topic 80: Respect

"I firmly believe that respect is a lot more important,
and a lot greater, than popularity."

Source: Julius Erving

We all feel the need to be popular, but you cannot let that desire stand in the way of doing the right thing. Doing the right thing will not always make you popular.

Accept the differences in race, ethnic background, sexual orientation, political views, etc., and grant everyone the respect they deserve as valuable team members. Only judge them on their contribution to both your success and your organization's success. Uncle Tony always believed that the respect you receive is equal to the respect that you give.

Speaking of respect, Uncle Tony once attended a seminar on respect. The seminar leader said to one of the attendees, "Imagine you have died, and as people walked up to your casket, what would you like to hear them say about you?"

One attendee said, "I would like to hear them say that I was a great family man."

The seminar leader asked a second attendee, "And what would you like to hear people say about you as they walked up to your casket?"

The second attendee said, "I would like to hear them say that I was a great manager."

The seminar leader next approached Uncle Tony and said, "What would you like to hear people say as they walked up to your casket?"

Uncle Tony said, "I would like to hear them say, look, he is moving."

Topic 81: Results

"Don't tell me about your effort,
show me your results."

Source: Tim Fargo

How often do you hear that it is the effort and not the results that count? Uncle Tony would disagree when it comes to the business environment. Sure, effort leads to results, and the harder you try, the more likely it is that you will have better results. But in the end, it is the results that count.

Some people in the business world seem to be confused about the relationship of effort and result, thinking effort is what is important. They talk about working through lunch, arriving early, staying late, or both. That is all fine and good, but only if it improves results. So often, it doesn't. It isn't how hard someone works; it is the results they produce.

While on the topic of results, you need to be measuring your results, since you usually get what you measure. You need to be absolutely certain that you are measuring what matters and not simply what is easy to measure. For instance, it is often easy to monitor how many hours a team member puts in during a week. What you want to be measuring is that person's output during the week and the quality of that output. Also, be sure to involve your team members in the setting of measurements, since they have firsthand insight to many of the processes you need to measure.

Keep in mind that many routine day-to-day activities aren't worth measuring. As Uncle Tony used to ask, "Is the juice worth the squeeze?" Even if you are measuring critical processes, it is good to take a reality check every so often to make sure you are reaching your overall desired outcomes.

Talking about effort and results, I knew Uncle Tony had joined a gym six months ago. When I saw him, I said, "I know you joined a gym, but you don't look any different. Why?"

Uncle Tony said, "You're right, I don't look or feel any different. I think I am going to have to drop by that gym and see personally what is going on in that place."

Topic 82: Retirement

"The best time to start thinking about your retirement
is before the boss does."

Source: Unknown

Uncle Tony said, "Always leave them wanting more." That is probably true of about everything, and it is especially true of leadership. You want to leave on a high note, with people wishing you were staying longer.

You certainly don't want people saying or even thinking it is time for you to retire, or worse yet that you should have left long ago.

So, you need to have a plan, perhaps a ten-year plan, for your expected retirement date. Pick a retirement date, and then work backward, identifying various milestones so that you can tell if you are on course for retirement or if you need to take corrective action. This is one time when long-range planning makes sense.

When you do retire, that is it—leave! Don't try to influence things after you are gone. Your time is up; let others have their time.

If you feel you must pass on some advice to whoever is coming into your position upon your retirement, here is some advice from Uncle Tony:

Uncle Tony suggests you prepare three letters for your replacement with instructions to open the first letter should they get into big trouble. The first letter says, "Blame everything on your predecessor."

If they get into big trouble again, the second letter says, "Reorganize."

And if they get into big trouble a third time, the third letter says, "Prepare three letters.

Topic 83: Rotation

"Intelligence is the ability to adapt to change."

Source: Stephen Hawking

Job rotation is a management approach of moving team members from one position to another at set intervals. Among its benefits are giving team members a broader view of the corporation so they can perform better and also provide backup when needed. For jobs of a more routine nature, it may reduce the monotony of the work. Job enrichment, on the other hand, is adding responsibilities from higher-ranking jobs to a person's current responsibilities. Either way, it involves change.

Both approaches can lead to employee stress and wasted time learning another job or higher-level responsibilities. Most people are better at some things than they are at others, or just happy doing what they are doing. I suspect it works better for management-rotation programs, where the aim is to prepare someone for an executive position, than it works for line-area operations.

Uncle Tony thinks you should let the employee decide if they want to take part in a job-rotation program or a job-enrichment program. As for you, if you have the option, it would be wise to volunteer for such programs. It is good to learn all you can about your organization, before taking on higher-level responsibilities.

After hearing Uncle Tony's recommendation about job rotation, I asked him, "So you like rotation?"

Uncle Tony said, "When it comes to rotation, I like how the Earth rotates. It makes my day."

Topic 84: Secrets

"If you would keep your secret from an enemy,
tell it not to a friend."

Source: Benjamin Franklin

Uncle Tony always said, "Two people can keep a secret, so long as one of them is dead." In other words, the only way to keep a secret is to not tell anyone. I'm not sure how many times Uncle Tony was told, "Anything you say can and will be used against you." It is a good warning for those entering the corporate world.

If you don't want people to know something about you, then don't tell anyone. Worst of all, do not put anything in writing or on social media that you would not want to see in headlines in the next morning's newspaper.

In the course of your life and corporate career, you are probably going to do something or say something you will later wish you hadn't. I suspect everyone has; but some people are better at keeping secrets than others.

While on the topic of secrets, I recall Uncle Tony asking me, "Why can't banks keep secrets?"

I replied, "I don't know."

Uncle Tony said, "Because they have too many tellers."

Topic 85: Self-Control

"I cannot trust a [person] to control others
who cannot control [themselves]."

Source: Robert E. Lee

You do not want a reputation as a hothead. You must always remain in control of yourself. Yes, on rare occasions, choosing to display your anger could forcefully drive a point home. Note the word, "choosing," which means you were in control of your anger but decided to let it show. Please don't overuse this tactic.

Uncle Tony used to say that the best way to win a fight, and he won many, was to get your opponent to lose control. When you lose control, you can't think straight. If you do not have self-control, you will undo all your efforts to get ahead. Usually, an angry person looks like a fool. Plus, you must have self-control to keep your vices in check; otherwise, they will be your undoing. Remember, you must always remain in control of yourself.

Don't let trifles undo your reputation for composure. It will often be tiny annoyances that will be what may get to you in an unguarded moment.

Uncle Tony claimed that his second wife was a model of self-control. No matter how mad he got, she would always remain calm. He could never figure it out, so one day he asked her, "How do you remain so calm, when I get so angry?"

She said, "I just go and clean the toilet."

Curious, Uncle Tony said, "And how does that help?"

She replied, "I clean it with your toothbrush."

Topic 86: Skills

"The future belongs to those who learn more skills
and combine them in creative ways."

Source: Robert Greene

Uncle Tony believed you should continuously upgrade your skills. It is great if you can get your organization to pay for your training. If that isn't going to happen, then invest in yourself. You will reap the dividends. Select the appropriate training for where you are in the corporation and for your next step up the ladder.

Be sure to embrace technology, at least to the point of knowing about it and as much as possible being able to make use of it. You want to be a bit more than current with technology, but not so far that you find yourself on the cutting edge of technology. Uncle Tony used to refer to those who went to the cutting edge of technology, which was often unreliable and costly, as being on the bleeding edge of technology.

Don't neglect reading as a way to stay sharp. Include more than just leadership books or books on your specialty. You can find many creative ideas in other types of books that you can creatively adapt to your own situation.

Speaking of skills, one day Uncle Tony told me, "I have good parking skills."

I replied, "What makes you say that?"

Uncle Tony replied, "Because the other day a police officer gave me a ticket and it said 'Parking Fine.'"

Topic 87: Succession

"Succession planning often results in the selection
of a weaker version of yourself."

Source: Peter Drucker

Uncle Tony thought the problem with formal succession planning is that it often becomes apparent who is going to be promoted. He thought the more people who felt they had a chance for promotion, the more productive your team would be. Besides, you probably already have an idea who is promotable. However, as much as possible, don't let it show.

If you are promoting people into positions that still will be reporting to you, you will have a great deal of influence but will likely still need buy-in from the level above you. This should not be a problem, if your candidate is worthy and you have done a good job of showcasing their value over time. If you are getting a lot of pushback from the person you report to, consider that they may be keeping you from making a mistake.

As for your own replacement, you will likely have some influence; but expect that the final decision will come from whom your replacement will report to, which is only right.

Uncle Tony thought loyalty is the number one criteria for selecting someone who will report to you. They don't have to be super talented, just someone who can do the job. Don't be foolish and advance a sharp, hungry tiger, since they will eventually be coming after you.

Uncle Tony once told me about an older friend of his who was retiring from a successful business he had built over many years

His friend called in an employee and told the employee, "You came here three years ago and started in the mail room. A year later, I made you sales manager. The following year, I promoted you to vice-president of sales. I'm retiring this year and I am going to make you president of the company. What do you say to that?"

The employee said, "Thank you."

Tony's friend said, "Thank you. Is that all you have to say?"

The employee said, "Thank you dad."

Topic 88: Team

"We are not a team because we work together.
We are a team because we respect, trust and care for
one another."

Source: Vala Afshar

Uncle Tony thought that all the members of your team are volunteers and you should treat them as such. He said, "They are volunteers because, though you can get them to stay at their desks, you can't force them to give their best." They will volunteer their best if they believe you respect them, if you treat them fairly, and especially if you make it clear that you appreciate their efforts.

One way of demonstrating your respect for them is to go to their workstation if you need to speak to them. If, for some reason, they need to come to your office, you should always let them know the reason for the request. This prevents them from speculating as to why you want to see them.

In terms of team size, you are always better off with a few good team members than a large number of mediocre or indifferent workers. Most likely you will have to work with the team you have inherited when you came into the position. If you feel your team is too large, often attrition is the solution. If you feel your team is too small, you must use facts to build a case for more team members. If the team lacks cohesion, this is where you prove yourself as a leader.

It is good to be friendly and to get to know your team members on a personal basis, just not too friendly, and certainly don't make them your confidant. Always remember familiarity breeds contempt.

You want to be fair to your team members, but don't make the common mistake of trying to be fair by treating all your staff the same. Uncle Tony used to say, "One rule for the horse and one rule for the cow is unfair to both." With that said, you must always take into consideration the impact of your treatment of one team member on the other members of your team.

Never ever make the mistake of using fear to motivate staff. Fear paralyzes people and keeps them from acting or causes them to act in a foolish way, different from how they would have acted without the influence of fear. Staff will perform, if they respect you and know you are always looking out for them. They, in turn, will look out for you.

I was talking to Uncle Tony about team building, when he asked me, "Why do you think a team would ask a tiny ghost to join their team?"

I said, "I have no idea."

Uncle Tony said, "Because they needed a little team spirit."

Topic 89: Telephone

"You should not be a slave to your telephone.
The technology is there to serve you,
not the other way around."

Source: Martin Cooper

Uncle Tony insisted that the primary rule when it comes to phone etiquette is this: If you are in a meeting or talking to someone, do not stop and answer the phone. This is also true for texting and emailing.

Before you go into a meeting or if you are having a lunch with a business associate, you should set your phone to silent/vibrate. There is nothing wrong with letting your phone go to voicemail. Afterward, you can listen to the voicemail and take appropriate action. Uncle Tony told me that he had actually heard people take a cell phone call during a funeral service and say that they can't talk right now. He always wondered what was the point of saying you can't talk right now. They should have simply let the call go to voicemail.

If for some reason you are not going to be able to access your messages, it is only courteous to leave an out-of-office or unavailable message letting the caller know when you will once again become available.

On rare occasions, you may know you will soon be receiving an important call. Let the party you are speaking to know at the start of the conversation that you will have to take this call, and ask if that is okay with them or if they want to have their conversation later.

Uncle Tony never understood those people who have to be on their phones all the time. You know who these people are, so don't be one of them.

If the topic to be discussed is sensitive, one that could develop into an argument, you want to have the conversation in person. Phone conversations tend to bring out the worst in people if there is a disagreement.

Speaking of telephones, one day Uncle Tony asked me, "How does a telephone propose to its girlfriend?"

I said, "I don't know."

Uncle Tony replied, "The telephone gives the girl a ring."

Topic 90: Terminations

"Dealing with employee issues can be difficult,
but not dealing with them can be worse."

Source: Paul Foster

Uncle Tony thought you were never doing anyone a favor, keeping employees who cannot perform their job. These employees may not want to lose their job. They know they aren't up to the job and so never feel good about themselves. Plus, you burden your productive employees with carrying the load of these low-performing workers.

Of course, before terminating, you need to make sure you have made every effort to bring them up to speed. You need to have made it clear to them over a significant period of time that their performance is considerably below expectations. You also need to get your human resources area involved as early in the process as possible. But remember, it is a rarity that a cooperative and willing employee doesn't possess some skills that, if not useful in your area, may be most useful in another area.

There is another type of employee who needs to go, not because of their performance, but because they are relentless in trying to undermine your authority and even destroy you. This sometimes happens if you are coming into a new area. It is likely someone will challenge your authority to lead the group. Typically, it is a single person that is leading the rebellion. The longer you wait to get rid of this person, the more you put yourself at risk.

When it came to incompetent or disgruntled team members, Uncle Tony used to say, "When did you ever hear someone say they wished they had waited longer to fire someone?"

Do your best to terminate employees with respect and try to get the best termination financial package you can for them, regardless of whether or not you like the particular person. Remember, your team will be watching how you treat these people and usually word gets out regarding how you let the person go.

On the positive side, sometimes getting fired is the spark you need to make some significant progress in your career. Uncle Tony told me years ago when he was a truck driver for Pepsi, he got fired.

I asked, "Why did they fire you?"

Uncle Tony said, "Because I tested positive for Coke."

Topic 91: Three

"If you want something stuck in someone's head,
put it in a sequence of three."

Source: Brian Clark

Have you ever heard of the Rule of Three? It is a principle that things in groups of three are simply more satisfying and complete than other numbers.

Uncle Tony advised that anytime you are giving reasons for something, just give your three strongest reasons. You can make use of this rule in a number of ways by just offering alternatives. For instance, if you are narrowing down candidates for a position, narrow it down to just three candidates.

If you will just look around you, you will see so many examples of the effective use of the Rule of Three, such as in children's stories like *The Three Little Pigs*. I'm sure you can find many more examples, and if you listen to effective speakers, you will hear how often they make use of the Rule of Three.

Uncle Tony told me that he first learned of the Rule of Three from his first girlfriend. She told him, "I just bought a three-piece bikini."

Uncle Tony said, "A three-piece bikini. That doesn't make sense."

She replied, "Sure it does. There is a top, a bottom, and a blindfold for you."

Topic 92: Time

"Time is the single most important resource that
we have. Every single minute we lose is never
coming back."

Source: Tarun Sharma

Uncle Tony thought time was one's most valuable resource and everyone gets the same 24 hours each day. The difference is what we make of each precious 24-hour day. He believed that one could accomplish so much if they used their time better.

The first step is that you must know how you are spending your time. The only way to know that is to log your time as you are doing things and not simply rely on your memory. You need to do this time-recording procedure every so often. Then study your time log and see what unproductive or low-value activities you are engaging in. Either stop them, delegate them, or pay someone to do them.

Always remember the best time-management tool is the word "No." It is amazing how much time one can free up to do things that are important, just by not being afraid to use this word.

Speaking of time, I recall Uncle Tony asking me, "What time is it when an elephant sits on your car?"

I replied, "I don't know. What time is it?"

Uncle Tony said, "It's time to get a new car."

Topic 93: Training

"The only thing worse than training your employees
and having them leave
is not training them and having them stay."

Source: Henry Ford

Uncle Tony believed that the training you provided to your team is a double-edged sword, sometimes helpful and sometimes worthless. Even when it is helpful, it isn't unheard of for an employee to use the knowledge gained to find another job. You probably should make certain the training relates to their current position or a position you plan to promote them to in your current area.

You should never use training as a reward; there are far better ways to reward an employee than sending the person to a training program.

And please don't use training, such as dispute-resolution skills, to fix a personality issue. It simply doesn't work. They will be the same person when they return. It is rare that a person can change, even when they want to change. If possible, find a position where the person's personality will be a better fit. Uncle Tony used an extreme example to make the point. He would say, "A person with an extremely forceful personality may not be the best grief counselor; however, that same person may make an excellent Army drill sergeant."

Every so often you will see a need to provide your team with training. You should carefully select the right training and the right team members to make the best use of your training dollars.

Just as important, don't neglect your own training. If your company will not pay for it, pay for it yourself. Actually, that is a good rule for training: If you or your employees would be willing to pay for it out of their own pocket, it is probably worthwhile training. If you or your employees aren't willing to spend their own money on the training, it probably isn't of good value.

Uncle Tony told me this story about one of his buddies, who was in the Army.

The sergeant said to Uncle Tony's buddy, "Hey soldier, I didn't see you at camouflage training this morning."

The soldier replied, "Thank you very much, sergeant."

Topic 94: Trust

"He who does not trust enough will not be trusted."

Source: Lao Tzu

In business as in life, Uncle Tony knew that there will be times when people you totally trust will disappoint you or even betray you. Uncle Tony always forgave them but didn't forget who they were. He also thought there would be a few that you should be willing to trust again. In doing so, you may find your most loyal supporters.

It is a sorry person, as well as an unsuccessful person, who trusts no one. Still, you must be cautious regarding those you trust, choosing wisely after studying their natures. Even then, over time, you will experience disappointments.

Uncle Tony enjoyed repeating this story that relates to the basic nature of some people:

A scorpion, being a poor swimmer, asks a turtle to carry him on his back across a river.

The turtle replies, "Do you think I am crazy? You will sting me and kill me, while I am carrying you across the river."

The scorpion replies, "I would never do that because if I stung you, then I would drown in the river."

The turtle says, "I guess you are right. So, hop on my back."

The scorpion climbs on the turtle's back and halfway across the river, the scorpion stings the turtle.

The turtle cries out, "Why did you do that? Now we are both going to drown."

The drowning scorpion says, "It's just my nature."

Topic 95: Turnover

"Managers tend to blame their turnover problems on
everything under the sun,
while ignoring the crux of the matter:
people don't leave jobs; they leave managers."

Source: Travis Bradberry

Turnover is expected when new management comes in to an under-performing area to shake it up. You can also expect some turnover due to promotions and various personal reasons.

However, it is pretty easy to recognize excessive turnover—and the reason for excessive turnover is almost always management, except in extreme circumstances that are also reasonably easy to recognize.

Poor management will always make a case that their excessive turnover is outside of their control and, of course, their excuses will sound plausible. Uncle Tony thought the real reason, though, is that they are either hiring poorly or treating their team members poorly. You need to investigate why there is exceptionally high turnover.

Uncle Tony asked me, "When someone quits their job at Apple, what is that called?"

I said, "What do you mean, what is it called?"

Uncle Tony grinned and said, "It's called Apple turnover."

Topic 96: Vacations

"A vacation is what you take
when you can no longer take
what you've been taking."

Source: Earl Wilson

Uncle Tony believed that vacations are an absolute must. Everyone needs to get out of the work environment for a period of time to recharge. Plus, often the time away from work may give a person a fresh perspective on how to do the work better upon their return. A less positive reason why people should be required to take vacations is that it is a fraud-prevention tool. People engaged in fraudulent activities typically need to be in the workplace to keep their activities from surfacing.

There are those who feel their vacation time is sacred. Nevertheless, you should still be reachable via email, text, or phone by whomever you left in charge. There is always the possibility of a business emergency or something of a critical personal nature that you need to know about.

The key is to leave someone in charge who can make decisions and whose judgment you trust. They will not intrude upon your vacation unless it is necessary.

When it comes to vacations, Uncle Tony said, "A journey of a thousand miles begins with a cash advance."

Topic 97: Values

"Watch your thoughts,
They become your words.
Watch your words,
They become your actions.
Watch your actions,
They become your habits.
Watch your habits,
They become your character.
Watch your character,
It becomes your destiny."

Source: Lao Tzu

Uncle Tony thought a leader needed to have deep-rooted values and not just utter phrases that sound good to your team and others. Your thoughts, your words, and your actions must reflect the values you hold dear. It is up to you to choose those values, and choose them with great care.

Once you have firmly identified your values, select those appropriate to advocate in the workplace, since some values are of such a personal nature that you have no right to push them on to your team members. Once you have identified your workplace values, you must train your team in them.

You cannot be everywhere and involved in every act. Therefore, the workplace values you lay out are guides to thinking, and every one of your team members must know them well and take them to heart. When that is accomplished, you can trust your team to act independently of you.

Uncle Tony told me that he didn't initially understand the value of his first wife.

I asked, "What changed?"

Uncle Tony said, "When the judge told me how much I was going to have to pay in alimony."

Topic 98: Visualization

"If you want to reach a goal,
you must 'see the reaching' in your own mind
before you actually arrive at your goal."

Source: Zig Ziglar

Uncle Tony thought you needed to take every opportunity to imagine yourself in the situation you seek. Think about it whenever you have a little free time or at night when you are about to go to sleep. Wake up and take a moment to think about it again. Each time, try to visualize the situation in greater detail.

Remember, if you can't even imagine something, it is unlikely to happen. Many staff people cannot visualize themselves as anything other than staff. You have to see yourself as someone who already possesses leadership traits and act accordingly. You want to avoid any negative self-talk or thinking, since that is just another form of failing to visualize yourself in the situation you desire.

Once Uncle Tony told me he was dating a girl from another nation.

I asked, "What nation?"

Uncle Tony laughed and said, "My imagination."

Topic 99: Volunteer

"The nicest feeling in the world is to do a good deed
anonymously and have somebody find out."

Source: Oscar Wilde

Uncle Tony never liked the idea of companies donating money to charities or even having their employees do charity work on company time. He thought that ultimately, the true cost of corporate charity comes out of the pockets of their customers.

However, Uncle Tony was a realist. Given today's political environment, you need to wholeheartedly support corporate volunteering and keep your personal opinion to yourself. A good way to demonstrate your leadership skills is to volunteer to head up a charity event or, even better, come up with an idea for a charity event that you can lead. If you can get others to help you with the charity event, it will demonstrate your team-building skills.

I remember Uncle Tony telling me that his first wife told him that she was concerned about women who were starving. She said, "I'm going to donate all the clothes I no longer wear to a charity that helps starving women."

Uncle Tony replied, "If any of your clothes fit them, they are definitely not starving."

Final Thought - Desiderata

Desiderata by Max Ehrmann

Go placidly amid the noise and haste, and remember what peace there
may be in silence.

As far as possible without surrender be on good terms with all persons.

Speak your truth quietly and clearly; and listen to others, even the dull
and the ignorant; they too have their story.
Avoid loud and aggressive persons; they are vexations to the spirit.

If you compare yourself with others,
you may become vain and bitter; for always there will be greater and
lesser persons than yourself.

Enjoy your achievements as well as your plans.
Keep interested in your own career, however humble; it is a real pos-
session in the changing fortunes of time.

Exercise caution in your business affairs,
for the world is full of trickery.
But let this not blind you to what virtue there is;
many persons strive for high ideals; and everywhere life is full of
heroism.

Be yourself.

Especially, do not feign affection.
Neither be cynical about love, for in the face of all aridity and disen-
chantment it is as perennial as the grass.

Take kindly the counsel of the years, gracefully surrendering the
things of youth.

Nurture strength of spirit to shield you in sudden misfortune.
But do not distress yourself with dark imaginings.
Many fears are born of fatigue and loneliness.

Beyond a wholesome discipline, be gentle with yourself.

You are a child of the universe, no less than the trees and the stars; you
have a right to be here.
And whether or not it is clear to you, no doubt the universe is unfold-
ing, as it should.

Therefore, be at peace with God, whatever you conceive Him to be,
and whatever your labors and aspirations, in the noisy confusion of life
keep peace with your soul.

With all its sham, drudgery, and broken dreams,
it is still a beautiful world. Be cheerful.
Strive to be happy.

Conclusion

Thank you very much for taking the time to read this book or even glancing at this page.

I've tried to price this book so that anyone can afford to take a chance that this book may benefit them.

I wish you the best in your future endeavors.

And finally, I leave you with these words:

"I long to accomplish a great and noble task,
but it is my chief duty to accomplish humble tasks
as if they were great and noble.

The world is moved along
not only by the mighty shoves of its heroes,
but also by the aggregate of the tiny pushes
of each honest worker."

Source: Helen Keller

Acknowledgements

Obviously, this book would have never been possible without Uncle Tony. There were four other people who also made this book possible.

Carol Allen

My wife of many years, who reviewed every page of this book a number of times. She is a retired school teacher and world-renowned gin and tonic mixer.

Chris Doka

A great friend and a great editor, who one day is going to become very famous. She has more than 10 years of experience line editing, copy editing, and proofreading everything from books and magazines to websites and content marketing materials. Chris can be reached at chris.doka@gmail.com

Tania Jann

A great friend and great motivator, who has considerable management experience and provided numerous insights to the topics in this book. She is most well known as being the World's Best Mom to her daughters Harmony and Lindsey.

Tony Russo

No, he isn't Uncle Tony; but he made significant contributions to so many of the topics covered in this book. He is without a doubt one of the very best managers I have ever come across, and I am sure anyone who ever reported to Tony would agree.

www.ingramcontent.com/pod-product-compliance
Lightning Source LLC
Chambersburg PA
CBHW051833090426
42736CB00011B/1780